ORDER UP!

THE INS AND OUTS
OF GETTING YOUR
FOOD TRUCK
EMPIRE ON THE ROAD

DIANN SEIBERT

© 2020 Order up! The ins and outs of getting your food truck empire on the road
All rights reserved. No part of the book may be reproduced in any shape or form without permission from the publisher.

This guide is written from a combination of experience and high-level research. Even though we have done our best to ensure this book is accurate and up to date, there are no guarantees to the accuracy or completeness of the contents herein.

This book has been designed using resources from unsplash.com and www.pexels.com.
ISBN: 978-1-953714-34-3

Reviews

Reviews and feedback help improve this book and the author. If you enjoy this book, we would greatly appreciate it if you could take a few moments to share your opinion and post a review on Amazon.

Contents

Introduction — 7

Section 1 Food Truck 101: The Basics — 11

    Chapter 1 The Fantastic History of Food Trucks — 12

    Chapter 2 Food Trucks Today — 15

    Chapter 4 Having a Food Truck Business vs. a Restaurant — 23

        Location — 23

        Travel — 25

        Weather — 26

        Responsibility — 27

        Size — 28

Section 2 Building Your Food Truck : Out of the Blueprints and into the Fryer — 33

    Chapter 1 What Will You Serve? — 34

        Choosing Your Menu — 38

        A Word About Beverages — 43

    Chapter 2 How Will You Prep, Cook, and Serve Your Products? — 48

        Hot Food Service Equipment — 49

        Elements of Refrigeration — 53

        Cooking Gear and Storage — 54

        Serving Gear — 57

    Chapter 3 Food Truck Biomechanics — 61

        Getting It Together: Prep Space and Sinks — 61

        Making It All Work: Ventilation, Generators, and Fuel — 66

    In Summary — 69

Section 3 The Business of Making Dreams Come True : Forming Plans and Buying Pans — 73

   Chapter 1 Creating a Business Plan — 73

      Finding the Money — 75

      The Legal Stuff — 78

      Chapter 2 Choosing Your Chariot — 80

      Finding and Purchasing — 80

      General Maintenance — 85

      Storing — 87

   Chapter 3 Cooking Up Connections — 88

      Suppliers — 89

      Staff — 92

      Commissaries — 94

   Chapter 4 Considering Your Operations Strategy — 95

      Processes — 95

      Set Up, Serve, And Strike — 97

      Safety — 98

Section 4 Turning a Business into a Brand : Establishing Yourself and Making Profit — 101

   Chapter 1 Building Your Brand — 101

   Chapter 2 Designing Your Marketing Plan — 104

   Chapter 3 Selecting Your Venues — 107

Conclusion — 110

Resources — 112

Introduction

Not too long ago, you had to look carefully or you'd miss it. If you were lucky, you could find one hanging out at the local corner shop. Weekends were usually a little easier. With so many people out and about, it didn't take too much effort to find what you were looking for.

Usually, you'd know you were close by taking a deep whiff of the air. The scents would just linger on the breeze. You'd inch closer and closer, salivating as the excitement grew, and you'd know you were so close to satisfying all of those urges.

And the waiting was terrible. This happened so rarely, and it was such an event, that you'd bounce restlessly, the change in your pocket jingling as you impatiently shifted from foot to foot, willing your favorite dish to still be available once you got to the front of the line.

But wasn't the pay off so very, very sweet? Wrapping your hands around that steaming hot delectable dish that you could only buy at your favorite food truck has always been a rewarding experience for the senses, the emotions, and, of course, the appetite.

Today, it's much easier to find a food truck. No longer relegated to cornershop parking lots or the street corners of weekend urban playgrounds, food trucks today pop up at small businesses, breweries or wineries, hardware stores, and even in larger neighborhoods. In fact, if you search online for "food trucks near me," chances are good that the nearest urban or suburban area will have quite a few options to try.

A food truck frenzy is quickly sweeping the nation, with new and exciting flavors appearing in communities all the time. There's no sign that this is a mere trend, either. Though it's impossible to know exactly how many food trucks are in service at any given time, reports indicate that there are around 25,000 food trucks in operation around the United States. And given two food trucks are rarely identical, even though they may serve the same dish, this means there are 25,000 exciting culinary adventures roaming the streets of this country just waiting to be discovered.

The name of the game when it comes to food trucks is "opportunity." This word fits both the experience of the customers, who are given the opportunity to try new foods and flavors that might otherwise never have been known to them, and the food truck operator, who has the opportunity to share their favorite cuisine with their community.

The idea of "opportunity" resonates throughout the food truck community. There is, of course, the ability to earn a profit, to mobilize your business to attract the customers needed to keep your food truck afloat. A smaller-scale operation like a food truck gives restaurateurs a low-risk scenario in which they can try out new dishes and new concepts, as well. Plus, for those who love a good adventure, a traveling restaurant can provide an amazing way to interact with your community and beyond. You're only limited by how vast your dreams are, and how far your wheels can take you.

In this book, we'll explore the possibilities, potential, and realities of food trucks. We'll start with an introduction to the basics of food trucks. While some readers might be extremely familiar with the ins and outs of food trucks, some of you might be exploring this topic with a fresh eye. So pull up a chair and we'll tuck in to the history, the ideals, and the purpose of a food truck.

Once we've explored the evolution of the modern food truck, you should feel more inspired than ever to get your own model running. Therefore, we'll take a moment to look at how food trucks work. They are more than a truck with a microwave in the back. You might not have considered how to change the grease in a mobile fryer or how a refrigerator on a trailer keeps things cool. We'll investigate all of those details.

From there, we'll dive into making your food truck dreams come to life. By the end of this book, you should be comfortable creating a business plan for your future food truck, and have some good ideas about what to serve, how to serve it, and a few more ideas to help you drive off into the sunset with the food truck business you are so eager to create.

You're going to have a lot of work ahead of you, but the good news is that you can have your cake, or your tacos, noodles, smoothies…any type of cuisine you can dream of, and eat it too.

There is a Resources section at the end of this book, where you'll find links to additional information on all of the topics mentioned throughout this book. Since every food truck is unique -- and every location may have different requirements -- it wouldn't be possible or practical to include all the details that might be specific to your food truck and location. However, we've rounded up the resources you'll need to get those details.

Additionally, as much as I've tried to be "evergreen" in this book, laws, regulations, and permit requirements change frequently. This book will lean towards operating a food truck business in the United States, but food trucks are absolutely not limited to the U.S. In fact, food trucks are cultural icons in many parts of the world, and will likely have far different requirements and trends than in the US.

While this book is intended to be as inclusive as possible of various scenarios and dreams, always check with local resources to ensure you're meeting all of the necessary guidelines.

Just as you waited in line for what seemed like an eternity for that rare, delicious food truck treat, there will be a lot of patience and planning involved with your future food truck enterprise. However, just as that long queue paid off every time, so will this wait. With your new food truck come loads of opportunity, which can lead to a lifetime of new experiences.

Section 1 Food Truck 101: The Basics

Before we explore your food truck and start making business plans for your new endeavor, let's pause to look at what a food truck really is. There are quite a few different types of "mobile food vending experiences," so as you're getting started, you will want to pause to consider which option best fits your vision.

We all come from different backgrounds and have a different understanding of what a food truck is or should be. For me, a food truck is a hot, greasy box filled with lots of hustle and excitement. Growing up, my grandparents had several what they called "concession stands." One sold just hotdogs and popcorn while the other truck was outfitted to sell elephant ears and funnel cakes. They spent the warm months traveling around our home state of Ohio, stopping at all sorts of outdoor events. From county fairs, to rummage sales, to lawnmower races, they did it all. When school let out for the summer, I loved joining them on the road for as long as my parents would let me.

Based on my experiences, I didn't really understand the hype about food trucks in my adult years. In college, my friends got super excited when we'd have food trucks on the quad. At first, I was confused. We had hot dogs in the school cafeteria, so why on earth would they be so stoked about that truck?

Bewildered, I joined them on the quad, and my attitude did a complete 180-degree turn. One of the food trucks featured **Bánh mì**, the popular Vietnamese sandwich. From another truck wafted the complex aroma of curry. Yet another sold baked potatoes the size of my face! Needless to say, this definitely opened my mind to what a food truck was and could be.

I tell this story to remind you to keep your mind very open when considering the possibilities for your food truck. Some readers are simply starting with the vague dream of owning a food truck, others have a very clear idea of exactly what they want to achieve. In either case, I urge you to learn about all the options before finalizing your business plan. Not every option is going to work for every situation.

I suppose I should preface this statement with the phrase "Spoiler Alert," but at the same time, it's good to get this out of the way early: Many of the decisions you make along the way will depend on the choices you've already made. That is to say, once you make one decision, it will trickle down and impact each upcoming step and choice yet to be made. Of course, life is pretty much like that, right? So let's take this one step at a time to avoid choice paralysis, confusion, or becoming overwhelmed.

Chapter 1 The Fantastic History of Food Trucks

I'm a firm believer that, in order to know where to go, you have to know where you've been. In this case, taking a look at the origins of food trucks will bring insight and ideas for creating your own version. Rather than reinventing the wheel, knowing the history of mobile food concessions can help make a few of your own choices clearer.

You might think of food trucks as a pretty recent invention, maybe even a product of the Industrial Revolution, when more and more men, women, and even children began to work long hours outside of the home. That's not a bad place to start, but it turns out that the idea of bringing food to the people, instead of the people to the food, started long before that.

From the chronicles of ancient Greek and Roman culture, we see evidence of street vendors providing sustenance to the more impoverished housing districts, where the homes did not have kitchens. The same practices were employed in ancient China, as well. It is theorized that street food predates the concept of restaurants in many areas, including Greece, Rome, China, and India. As urban areas developed so did the need for street food. The manner in which it was prepared and served continued to expand as well.

The first documented appearance of mobile food vending in the United States dates back to 1691. An influx of pushcart food vendors in New York

City brought about the need for regulations to avoid too much traffic congestion. Just a few years later, in 1707, the retail and restaurant industry in the city again complained that street food vendors were causing disruption to the public, to the flow of foot and horse-drawn traffic, and to their businesses. As a result, pushcart vendors were officially banned.

Of course, a quick look at New York City today shows us just how well that stuck. Rough estimates indicate there may be as many as 12,000-14,000 street food vendors within the city alone.

While these early entrepreneurs kept food-truckin' along despite the regulations to the contrary, the scene in the American West was similar...in the most different way possible. Westward movement and the expansion of cattle business meant lots of hungry cowpokes riding the range. The chuck wagon was developed by Charles Goodnight in 1866 as a way to keep cowboys and miners fed in the wild territory. While the earlier vendors sold prepared food from a moving cart, the chuck wagon featured all the means for storing, preparing, and cooking a full meal for many individuals. The operator, given the clever nickname of "Cookie," would typically prepare meals consisting of ingredients that travelled well over long distances, such as beans, coffee, potatoes, onions, and lard and flour to make biscuits. Of course, cattle were never too far away from the chuck wagon, so Cookie often knew many inventive ways to prepare beef.

One of the most interesting things about the chuck wagon is that it was truly intended as a fully operational kitchen on wheels. But instead of today's modern steel-and-aluminum vehicle fittings, everything had to fit onto a wagon. That meant reinforcing the axles with steel to navigate the unpredictable terrain, as well as fitting shelves, cabinets, flat prep surfaces, a water barrel, a coffee mill, and fuel for the Dutch oven, which was usually stored when not in use. A large trunk-like space known as the "chuck box" was typically built into the back of the wagon to provide a large flat surface as well as plenty of room for ingredients and larger supplies.

The next stop for the "food truck of days gone by" takes us to the lunch wagon. Invented by Walter Scott in 1872 as a response to the needs of hungry newspaper staff members in Providence, Rhode Island, Scott's take on the chuck wagon sold pre-packaged, prepared foods to the crowds.

Thomas H. Buckley decided to take this idea to the next level in the late 1880s. A former lunch-counter worker, he had a very acute understanding of the proper flow and prep needed for producing and serving fresh food to folks who were on a time crunch. His take on the lunch wagon included sinks, ovens, and refrigeration. These updates allowed wagon operators to expand their menus and their clientele. Buckley also made a few cosmetic changes, which allowed vendors to brand their wagons and add a little pizzazz to draw in the crowd.

This all occurred before the invention of automobiles. Anything with wheels had to be pushed by humans or pulled by horses. Streets were often paved in brick or stone, and dust, soot, and other debris were prevalent.

Around the same time, sausage vendors were becoming a popular fixture around the larger colleges and universities. Somehow bringing together all of these options into a single small vehicle, these "dog carts" sold one food: boiled hot dogs. But amazingly, the products were hot and fresh, and brought to the doorsteps of the dorms, where hungry students pounced on the chance for a quick, portable meal.

In 1917, the United States Army mobilized "field kitchens" to feed the troops. This delivery method essentially took the chuck wagon model and fit it within a motor vehicle. Add some U.S. Army practicality and efficiency and, by World War II, the concept expanded into a 2.5 ton freight vehicle that could feed hundreds of soldiers at a time.

While we commonly think of the food truck boom occurring more recently -- and certainly, if we think of the number of food trucks in commission across the country, that's true -- it was after World War II that mobile concessions found their place in the American lifestyle.
With the baby boom increasing the population, intrepid entrepreneurs combined marketing and a little mechanical know-how to bring us the

refrigerated ice cream truck, the famous Oscar Meyer Weinermobile, and what became somewhat affectionately known as "roach coaches," or mobile diners that catered specifically to construction and other labor-intensive work sites. Since workers at these sites couldn't just dash off for lunch breaks, "roach coaches" came to them, providing a captive customer base with a hot meal to keep them properly fueled throughout the day.

As roach coaches caught on, other rudimentary food trucks began to pop up through the 1970s and 1980s. Typically retro-fitted ice cream trucks, these "barf buggies," "gut trucks," "snack trucks," or "grease trucks" generally peddled one type of cuisine to industrial workers, construction sites, and college campuses. Wherever hungry people on a time crunch congregated, a mobile food vendor would be lurking nearby. In New York City, where this all began, hot dog carts seemed to pop up faster than flowers in the springtime. A dollar could get you a dog with all the fixings, perfect for snacking on the go.

But the history of the American food truck is just a microcosm of street food. As people immigrated to the United States, they brought with them the cuisine and traditions of their homelands.

In nearly all highly populated areas of the world, we see mobile food vendors preparing the traditional dishes of the area, adding convenience to the human need for hot, delicious food prepared and served in a timely manner.

Chapter 2 Food Trucks Today

In reviewing the history of food trucks, it's easy to see a lot of influences on today's food truck culture. In a sense, not much has changed. We still enjoy the convenience of mobile food vendors because the full restaurant experience isn't always conducive to our schedules or needs.
Of course, the overall technology of the food truck has evolved. While chuck wagons carried tinder and cow patties in a sling under the wagon, today's food trucks are fitted with generators and propane tanks that

power all sorts of modern conveniences, such as griddles, fryers, refrigerators, freezers, running water, and more.

One very interesting point is that the concept of the food truck has not changed tremendously over the years. The earlier pushcarts specialized in serving one dish to customers. Even though today's food trucks are certainly better equipped, the owners and operators stick with the concept of keeping it simple, focusing on a specific type of dish or cuisine. Several variants may be offered to accommodate a variety of diets and preferences but, typically, each food truck will focus on one specialty. For example, it would be unusual to find a gourmet baked potato on a taco truck. A food truck filled with exquisite cupcakes is highly unlikely to have a fryer full of corn dogs in the back.

At first glance, this might feel like a missed opportunity. After all, surely a well-placed food truck could sell anything, right? And surely, the more variety you have, the larger the customer base you can attract.

These are principles that work in larger settings. But in the cramped quarters of a food truck, storing, preparing, and serving too many different things would create a rift in the operational flow and a huge dent in the overhead costs. Even the most well-equipped 21st century chuck wagon will serve only a few different meals.

Another interesting concept that has evolved through history is the purpose and placement of food trucks in relation to different audiences. For example, the street vendors of the ancient world were dedicated to providing hot meals to the lower class, who would otherwise not have access to warm food. American mobile food developed along with the working class, following cowboys across the range, soldiers into the field, and construction workers to the site. And, increasingly, they are following urban workers to the office building.

Some modern food trucks, like the street vendors of ancient times, are always in the same place. They definitely have four wheels and an engine, but their location seems a bit permanent. Others appear completely unannounced in a parking lot, on a street, or in a neighborhood. Many food trucks are regularly scheduled to rotate between a few key locations or events. And some, like the first pushcarts of New York City, seem to be in constant motion.

Sometimes, a variety of food trucks will congregate. Many people have spent happy summers eating their way through a county or state fair. In some parts of the world, food trucks set up together along high traffic areas for those attending sporting events or simply out for a night of partying. Food truck festivals are a very modern take on this practice, with dozens of food trucks gathering in a central location to allow customers to sample the flavors from as many vendors as possible.

Of course, this is the 21st century, and technology and social media are here to help us find exactly what we want, when we want it. Food trucks are currently being celebrated for bringing delicious opportunities to many different locations, so we have devised technology to help us find our favorite vendors. We have created apps to track food trucks. In fact, some food trucks have apps that allow users to order their food from their home, their desk, or while out running errands so that they simply need to swing by and pick up their order at a designated time. Many modern food trucks in busy urban areas even offer delivery through sites such as GrubHub, UberEats, and DoorDash.

Many food trucks have their own Facebook and Instagram accounts, and some even send email alerts to customers letting them know when the truck will appear in their area. This not only helps people find the foods they crave, but it allows customers to generate a buzz about their favorites, posting pictures, comments, and sharing posts about each truck with their friends.

You'll want to consider all of these details and tidbits as you brainstorm your potential food truck. Do you want to create a chuck wagon with a permanent location, or a "roach coach" that shows up strategically at large corporations on pay day? Will delivery or apps be in your scope? Do you want to travel 100% of the time, or make this more of a side-hustle where you pick and choose venues that sound like a good investment of your time?

We'll go into deeper detail on each topic, including knowing what to serve, your mobile business model, and the ins and outs of marketing, but these little seeds of information are good to keep in mind as we dive deeper and deeper into the specifics of your food truck and business plan.

Chapter 3 What Is a Food Truck, Anyway?

When talking about the entire mobile food vending industry, there are many terms flung around. Sometimes these words are used interchangeably when they actually mean slightly different things.

As you are starting to piece together a few ideas about the specifications of your own food truck, you'll want to be as specific as possible about your plan, your goals, and the type of food stand you want. Let's look at a few different models of vendors that fall under the "food truck" umbrella, so you can get a better feel for what will best fit your dreams.

The first classification you'll need to know is "restricted" versus "unrestricted." "Restricted" means that the mobile food vendor is only licensed to sell food that has already been prepared and packaged. Examples include ice cream trucks, which sell individually-wrapped ice cream novelties, and the "roach coaches" mentioned earlier. Restricted food businesses prepare nothing onsite; they merely keep food warm or cold and distribute items as they are ordered.

"Unrestricted" means food items are prepared, cooked, and sold from a vehicle. Typically, these trucks have a home base or commissary they rely upon for cleaning, restocking, and regular maintenance. "Unrestricted" is somewhat of a misnomer, because there are loads of regulations placed on these types of trucks. For the purpose of this book, we'll largely focus on the requirements for an unrestricted business, though there will definitely be information appropriate for anyone interested in the mobile food business.

Even with those specifications, there are several options available for taking your food on the road. This table demonstrates some of the different types, specifications, and capabilities of mobile food vending units. In each category, there are loads of variances. The beauty of taking your restaurant on the road is that you still have the opportunity to customize it however you wish, so bear in mind that these are largely generalizations. We'll explore specifications as we plunge further into the construction and functionality details. At this stage in the planning process, the primary focus is on narrowing down certain things just a little bit at a time.

Type	Examples	Where to Find Them	Specifications
Street Cart	Hot dog cart, gyro cart, lemonade cart	- Frequently in motion; no established long-term spot	- Serves one type of food
		- Easy to set up at multiple locations within a day	- Limited customization
			- 5-6 feet in length
		- Outside bars and clubs, businesses, in parks	- Trailer behind a vehicle or manually pushed
			- Least expensive to purchase
			- Entirely outdoors
			- Potential for high volume of sales
			- Sales entirely dependent on finding a good location for operation
			- Operated by a single individual

Concession trailer	Fair food	- Specifically contracted for events or hired for a location - Fairs, festivals, large public events - May appear at a new location every day but remains in place for entire day	- Lightweight metal trailer - Folds into a closed cube - Very limited interior space - Does offer protection from the elements - 1-2 service windows to allow flow of traffic - Typical to add branding to the exterior walls, roof - Customer base drawn from the event/location 1-2 staff members per trailer, usually travel from location to location with the owner
Food truck	Your favorite cuisine to go!	- Hired to appear at specific locations or events for a specific period of time (eg- lunch hour at a large corporation) -Short term events (eg- concerts, weddings)	- Has a cabin area for a driver, and a food service area in the rear - Can be a large truck or bus - Features a service window - Limited space - Limited menu - Customer base is waiting at the location (limited outside exposure) - Owner operated with some help

Mobile Kitchen	Can be the mobile version of an established restaurant May be its own entity	- Elaborate set up - Typically found at long duration events such as state fairs, construction work sites, catastrophe relief - Slightly more permanent due to size	- Features a full kitchen - Room for prep, storage, and service - May include seating tent - Very large size means larger crowds can be served - Generally the only food service provider at location - Potential to provide variety of meals throughout the day - May offer delivery -Large staff to handle multiple tasks
Food Stand	Taco trucks, long term vendors	- Permanent or semi-permanent set up - Rarely moves - Found in parking lots, corner shops, gas stations, hardware stores	- May take the shape of a large truck or bus - Offers a variety of menu items - Devout following - May offer delivery - Semi-permanent staff

The purpose of this table is to loosely categorize the entire spectrum of mobile food vending options. There are tiny hot dog carts that haven't changed location in years, and there are elaborate southern-style smokehouse BBQ kitchens that set up at a new festival every weekend. There are overlapping ideas and concepts among the categories and no definition is set in stone.

One thing to bear in mind is that while there are definitely prefabricated carts, stands, and trucks, a lot of these vehicles are upfitted from a previous life as a cargo truck, a shipping container, a moving van, and, in some cases, you might find an actual garden shed on wheels serving as a food truck.

As you're starting to put weight behind your daydreams, a helpful exercise is to reflect on what you have personally seen and experienced. Consider the last time you went to a fair or festival. What types of concessions did you see on the midway -- or main thoroughfare -- of the grounds?

Chances are that you saw colorful awnings, giant signs, flashing lights, and waving flags excitedly beckoned you to step up and order funnel cakes, hot dogs, footlong corn dogs, blooming onions, cheese on a stick, and more. And then there were some slightly larger trailers offering more elaborate cuisine, such as bourbon chicken, cowboy stir fry, roast beef "sundaes" and the like, with a large grilling surface set up next to their trailer, where meats and veggies are constantly in various stages of sizzling in the open air. There might have been a kitchen unit from a local restaurant serving as the corner of a major intersection to foot traffic. Surrounded by a fence, there might be a large walk-through trailer serving food, with tables and chairs set up around the trailer itself. There might be a large tent, in which there are more tables, and possibly even live entertainment. And in the minority, but certainly holding their own, are a few gourmet food trucks selling fancy cupcakes, specialty coffees, or other local favorites otherwise not traditionally represented in the "fair food" category.

This particular scenario comes from my own experiences roaming around fairgrounds. Your experiences may be a bit different. And that is why, in these early stages before decisions are made, I encourage you to reflect upon the various types of food vendors you have seen and experienced.

Sometimes, when we're daydreaming about our ideal business venture, we can blend together many different aspects of several different existing business models. Sometimes that's the spark of innovation...but sometimes there's a reason why it hasn't been done before.

Since there are so many variables and options in the world of mobile food concessions, we're moving very slowly towards the process of constructing a business plan. Once you have started your business, it is very hard to modify the business plan mid-stream. As noted in the previous table, there are certain operating methods for each type of vending space, and while expansion is possible, nearly every food truck owner will tell you it is best to start with one operation, rather than running a whole fleet right out of the gate.

Tip-toeing through the first steps of creating your own food concession empire may seem tedious, but it is in these early steps that you are setting yourself up for long-term success. Don't worry; once your business plan is officially in motion, you'll likely have little time to rest, so enjoy the extra time to gather your thoughts now.

Chapter 4 Having a Food Truck Business vs. a Restaurant

The last thing we'll cover before we get into the "meat and potatoes" of starting your very own food truck business are the pros and cons of having a mobile food concession versus a brick and mortar restaurant.

Having been involved in both types of ventures, I prefer to look at these as "benefits" and "challenges," because both business models can be simultaneously successful and complicated. There is no "better" option, and there is certainly not an "easy" option. In fact, there are quite a few similarities throughout the process, especially in the food sourcing, storage, prep, and staffing areas. Many restaurateurs successfully make the switch from brick-and-mortar to mobile and back again, and some easily dabble in both enterprises. Therefore, let's look at some of the key points in which they differ, focusing on the specific benefits and challenges of running a food truck.

Location

You've probably heard the phrase "location, location, location," in reference to everything from opening a business of any kind, to purchasing a home, to marketing and beyond. A cactus might look cool on your coffee table, but if it doesn't get sunlight and warmth, it's not going to do well. Location matters.

Some say the biggest advantage of having a food truck is the flexibility of location. "You can go anywhere!" they say. "You can even hit multiple places a day!"

Traditional restaurants rely on customers coming to their location for the bulk of their business, with the occasional foray into catering, take out, or delivery as appropriate for their business model. Food trucks draw a crowd wherever they park. In many cases, the customer base is built into the location.

For example, you may have seen a food truck parked at a brewery that otherwise doesn't serve food. This creates a symbiotic relationship between the brewery and the food truck. Some customers come for the beer and stay for the food, others come for the food and stay for the beer.

This seems like the perfect plan, right? But there are a few key unpredictable factors that go into making this plan work exactly as anticipated. First, the brewery needs patrons. Maybe the brewery is hosting live music tonight and half the town has turned out to see the performer, drink the tasty libations, dance, have fun, and specifically eat your delicious food. Everyone wins. But what happens when the bar down the street has the live music, it's raining, and the brewery has run out of their most popular draft? In this instance, it's just another night for everyone involved.

In theory, a food truck could pack up and go wherever people are gathered, but it doesn't always work like that. Setting a food truck up is generally a lot more involved than parking and opening the service window, though admittedly, there are some specific trucks that have been designed with that exact business model. We'll walk through set up and strike in detail in a later chapter, but suffice it to say there are a number of steps and procedures that must be completed before anyone has food in their hands.

Therefore, while some trucks do appear at multiple locations in a day, it's not the norm. And while you can set up a food truck just about anywhere, there's a significant amount of thought and planning that goes into the process. You need to ensure that foot and vehicular traffic isn't impeded, that all the equipment can operate, and that you maximize the experience for everyone involved, from the owner of the food truck to the guy who just happened to be walking by and smelled something delicious.

Still, the ability to move as needed is an obvious overall benefit to the food truck operator. Even if you have a contract to work a fair for a few weeks, at the end of the contract, you can wander where the wind takes you.

Having this flexibility allows food truck vendors to make more informed decisions about the gigs they choose. Remember, if your business model is based on going TO the crowd, you will need to research the venues at which you park and the gigs you accept to ensure that the traffic will be worth the cost of operation. While you do have the benefit of moving your restaurant from place to place, once you're set up, you're attached to that spot for a significant amount of time.

Travel

Traveling itself can be both a benefit and a challenge. While having the wheels to spin and the roads to explore are very significant benefits, remember that traveling does have a price. You will need to keep your food truck well maintained and in good mechanical order. You also need to be prepared for the occasional breakdown, tire blowout, or traffic accident. Everyone has the best intention of driving cautiously and carefully and doing everything to keep their vehicle functioning perfectly, but accidents do happen. You'll need to fill up on gas when it runs low. Tires will need to be replaced. Oil changes will be needed, not just for the fryer, but for the engine as well. Everything you do for your daily driver car, you'll need to do for your food truck.

If you choose a concession trailer instead of a food truck or van, you'll also need a vehicle to pull it. That means maintenance for both the trailer and the vehicle, at least in making sure that the wheels, hitch, connectors, blinkers, lights, axles, and wiring are working appropriately when the trailer is on the road.

The amount of traveling you do directly impacts the amount of maintenance your vehicle or vehicles will require. Before you plan to travel all across your state, get a feel for gas prices and the maintenance requirements of your truck or trailer. If you want to do a lot of traveling, rather than taking advantage of the local market, be prepared to work the related expenses into your business plans.

This may seem obvious, but the food also has to travel. The general rules of food service safety indicate that cold ingredients must be kept below 40 degrees Fahrenheit, and hot food should be kept above 140 degrees Fahrenheit. We'll get into food safety in far more detail later, but temperatures in between 40-140 Fahrenheit are what the United States Department of Agriculture consider "The Danger Zone" in which bacteria are most likely to spread in food items. That means that if you have far to travel, you have to be very conscious about food storage.

Likewise, utensils and serveware are also along for the ride. Just as the chuckwagons of yore needed plenty of cabinets, drawers, and bins for storing everything that traveled the trails, your food truck needs to be equipped to securely hold everything that's hitting the road with you. You don't want to arrive at a gig with a truckful of scattered, dirty, and/or damaged serving containers. Without serving gear, you may not be able to actually work the gig as intended.

Weather

You may have noticed one particular factor in the earlier brewery example that no one can control: weather. Food trucks may provide shelter for the workers inside, but your customers will need to brave the elements in order to buy your wares.

Snow and rain will certainly deter customers from standing in line for a significant amount of time, no matter how delicious your food is. Thunderstorms and high winds can be downright dangerous, since food trucks are a combination of metal and movable pieces that can easily blow around and cause damage to someone or something. Weather that's bad enough can prevent traveling altogether.

Too much sun or heat and humidity can be an obstacle as well, but in this case, more for the people inside the truck. Food trucks require ventilation, but anyone who has worked in a commercial kitchen will tell you it gets very hot, very quickly. If you and your staff are running orders very quickly on a hot day, surrounded by hot grills and fryers, the chances for heat exhaustion or heat stroke increase very quickly.

There are things that can be done to mitigate against the weather, such as outdoor heaters along the queuing area when it's cold, water misting fans when it's hot, or a tent or awning over the service window for any weather condition. These elements are often dependent on what the venue can accommodate or allow, however. Some cities have regulations against where tents can be put up, and outdoor heaters may be against city ordinances as well.

Weather and the elements are indeed a huge factor in the food truck industry. And because the tools and equipment available to combat them can be expensive to purchase and run, many food trucks operate on a specific seasonal schedule.

Responsibility

As a food truck owner, you call the shots, and for most people, that's a huge benefit. If you only want to go out every other Saturday, that is your call. If you want to quit your day job and set up at a new place every day, it is certainly your prerogative.

In fact, you might feel like you're starting ahead of the curve by investing in a food truck instead of a brick-and-mortar restaurant. There's no rent or mortgage to pay, and no landlord to satisfy. You don't have to buy a dining room's worth of expensive chairs and tables or hire a decorator to do your colors and create an ambience. The overhead is initially lower, because you buy a vehicle, insert the equipment, and that's it, right?

Financially, there are risks and rewards every time you put the truck in park and fire up the propane. There's food cost, operating expenses, and travel expenses to balance with profit. You can only make money if you take the truck out and sell food. It's a classic "spend money to make money" scenario. And if you have a slow night, or that package of food containers spills during transit, or you drop a head of lettuce before you can chop it into individual salads, you've spent money that you're not getting back.

One sliver of a silver lining here, though, is that much of the money you take in is going right back to you and your business. Food trucks and mobile kitchens of all kinds have a far smaller staff than a standard restaurant. Even if you have a food runner, you do not have a full service staff. There are no cleaners or bussers. Due to lack of space, it would be impossible to have various stations, such as the line cook, prep cook, sous chef, expo., and kitchen manager. In a food truck, when the owner is also the head chef and working alongside staff, this means a dramatic reduction of payroll costs. And, if it's a solo operation, there are none. Minimal staff means minimal payout at the end of the night.

Size

While a small size and a small crew can be highly beneficial, there are a few places where it can be more of a challenge.

Having any number of people dashing about behind a small counter is going to be challenging, but just like any kitchen, you'll work out an intricate ballet over time. The key is to find the right balance between having available space in the kitchen and enough staff to prevent long wait times. Long wait times kill revenue, especially if there's a shorter and quicker line at the truck next to you.

Furthermore, that means you have to pack everything you can fit, and once you run out of anything, that's it. In some cases, it might be appropriate to run out and replenish stock. During the summer before I went to college, it seemed like there was a rush on hot dogs. I think my grandmother had me run out to buy more hot dogs at 90% of the stops we made that summer. While that was definitely a pain, hot dogs heat quickly, store easily, and are readily found just about anywhere. If your menu involves specialized ingredients or a particular brand, this might be difficult for you. Think ahead.

Less space means the ability to pack less food, less serving gear, and fewer supplies, which in turn means you have less product to sell. Selling less means making less money, and less money is less appealing.

Good news: there are ways to maximize your space so that your food truck makes financial sense. Limit your menu. Plan ahead. Keep impeccable records so you can look back and understand exactly what your weaknesses are. You need to consider space in all aspects of your business. You won't have a giant walk-in cooler to fill with all the meats and cheese you need, so you need to be very smart about everything that goes in the truck.

This is a significant amount of information to try to mull over at once, so to simplify, here's a "Benefits and Challenges" table. Think about your town, your preferences, and your idea for a food truck and come up with a few specific benefits and challenges of your own.

Benefits	Challenges
Can Park Anywhere	May be hard to find - hard to establish regulars
Can hit different locations/events daily	Travel results in wear and tear on vehicle and you
No mortgage/rent	Weather can slow down business
No seating area or large kitchen to maintain	Need to carefully plan all the details due to lack of space for extras
Lower overhead	Minimal storage
Very small staff	Very small staff

There are some instances in which a challenge may become a benefit, depending on your outlook and circumstances. For example, when my grandparents purchased their concession stands, the hot dog and popcorn trailer was fitted with equipment to install a beverage fountain, whereas the elephant ear and funnel cake trailer was not. While for some business plans, that might be a make-or-break situation, my grandparents were actually quite relieved to have only one fountain machine to deal with at a time. In fact, they took that as an opportunity to offer coffee out of the pastry stand. While this was a complete departure from their original plans, they were actually able to create a new opportunity out of this potential challenge.

As you create the business plan for your food truck, you'll find that the best laid plans are frequently waylaid. You will find yourself making urgent decisions, last minute "this won't work" recalculations, and all of the myriad other stressors that are born into existence when anyone decides to start a new business. The more you know heading into the experience, the less terrifying these decisions will become.

At this point, you might be daydreaming about a Texas cattle-drive themed sandwich truck, or maybe the earlier Bahn mi example got your attention, and you're doing a little math on how you might sell them from a pushcart. Or perhaps you're walking down the midway at the fair, taking note of how you might capture all the sights and flavors in your gourmet flavored popcorn stand.

From learning more about food truck culture, to exploring the different subtypes of food trucks, to weighing some of the basic benefits and challenges to running your own food truck, this section was designed to get those creative juices flowing.

In the next section, we'll get into a decision-by-decision plan for turning that dream into a reality. This is where you'll start making choices, like what type of food you'll make or the equipment you'll buy, and put it all together into a business plan. It's okay to start feeling excited and anxious. This is where things start to gel and feel real.

Section 2 Building Your Food Truck : Out of the Blueprints and into the Fryer

Much like the hot debate regarding the chicken and the egg, there can be some question as to which should come first: the food truck or the business plan. Some people feel you should purchase the food truck first, then create a theme, a menu, and a plan of action around what that food truck can do.

This can be a great course of action for those with established food truck businesses because these individuals have the expertise and insight into what their community can sustain, what food items work well in their area, the requirements for various locations, and so on.

For those starting with their very first food truck, however, I recommend starting with what you know and molding your plan and adapting your ideas as you go along. I've found that a significantly larger number of people who are interested in getting into the foodservice and hospitality industry in any capacity have a personal connection to the cuisine more than the actual method of delivery. It's also a commonly touted recommendation to follow your dreams and invest your time and energy into something that makes you feel passionate. As a result, it's far more common to hear plans for someone's first food truck start with "I want to open a food stand that sells my favorite dish," rather than "I really want a 200 square foot trailer equipped with a dual tank stainless steel 12-liter deep fryer."

The truth is that you'll have to do both, and we'll cover both parts of the process. However, for the purpose of this book, I have chosen to start with the dream aspect, which then moves at its own pace towards a real, tangible food truck, complete with all of the sights, smells, expenses, and joys that you have anticipated along the way.

Chapter 1 What Will You Serve?

A friend of mine, who has been an executive chef at a variety of fine dining establishments over the years, once said, "if you're going to devote all of your time and money to food, you better choose something you enjoy." While this advice can be applied to any career, it is essential in the food industry.

There are different levels of passion for food. First, there's an appreciation for a specific cuisine. You may love the bouquet of scents and flavors that come from a particular region or culture. Perhaps you are disappointed at the lack of a "scene" for that type of dish in your area and feel personally up to the challenge of opening the first option your community might have to taste these flavors.

An example of this is my good friend Linda's *dosa* truck. Growing up, she lived in a multicultural neighborhood. Some of her closest friends were from South India, and they introduced her to many of the elements of their culture. Linda fell in love with dosa, a type of thin crepe created from a fermented rice and lentil batter that is often stuffed with a savoury filling of potatoes, vegetables, cheese, or other ingredients.

As long as I have known her, Linda has been obsessed with dosa. She learned to make the dish on her own at a young age, and throughout her life, she has been more than happy to share the magic of dosa with everyone who stops by her house for a bite to eat. After college, she moved to a new city, and she was absolutely flabbergasted when she couldn't source a good dosa. She put both her dosa knowledge and her new college degree in accounting to work and started the very first dosa stand in her city.

In Linda's case, her primary motivation in opening her food truck was filling a specific niche with something she was passionate about. Her life-long love of a very specific dish has translated perfectly into the opportunity to share her passion with others, in the form of a food truck.

Another motivating factor behind choosing the menu for your food truck is your ability to plan and cook the food you intend to sell. Maybe there's a dish you make exceptionally well. Every time you get invited to a potluck or a party, you're specifically requested to bring this particular dish. When people come to your house for dinner, they expect this dish. Sure, you have a lot of culinary skill to bring to the table, but you have essentially become synonymous with this dish in the eyes of anyone who knows you.

My aunt used this strategy when creating her cheesecake-on-a-stick trailer. My aunt grew up on the road with my grandparents, so the concept of running a concession truck was very familiar to her. She never thought it was the life for her, though. She attended nursing school, became a nurse practitioner, raised my nieces, and put the mobile food business on the back burner.

However, my aunt makes an amazing cheesecake. Others in my family have attempted to copy her recipe, and it never works exactly right. She is required to bring a cheesecake to every family gathering, from holiday dinners to monthly game night.

One night, over a game of cribbage, someone remarked that she could put her children through college if she started selling her cheesecake regularly. One idea sparked another, and by the next year, she had figured out a way to prepare and freeze her cheesecake in such a way that she could sell it out of a concession trailer. There was a significant amount of innovation required to make cheesecake a food that would travel well. It turns out that her customers love her desserts as much as we do.

In my aunt's case, it made sense to monetize something she was already doing, and doing very well. She is passionate about making delicious desserts, but that's secondary to the fact that she is incredibly skilled. While Linda's motivation was giving more people the opportunity to try something amazing, my aunt's motivation was selling a quality product to supplement her income.

The next factor in determining what food you will sell is cost. What can you afford to buy or source? What prices will you have to charge to make a profit? Ingredients can be very expensive, depending on how intricate your recipes are. **If you put 45 ingredients in your soup, it will cost more than if you put 4 ingredients in your soup.** Additionally, some very tasty dishes require a significant amount of preparation, a specific manner of storage, and don't fit the "mobile" concept very well.

This was actually the largest motivating factor in my grandparents' choices for concessions. They aren't particularly passionate about hot dogs, and while I personally think my Pawpaw makes the best elephant ear I've ever had, there's nothing particularly special about it - it's just thin, fried dough that's been dipped in a heavy coating of cinnamon sugar at exactly the right moment to create a sweet, crispy glaze.

When creating their business model, my grandparents chose foods that can be purchased in bulk, stored simply, prepared easily, and sold quickly. People think nothing of paying $7 for a massive bag of salty, buttery popcorn that they can nibble on all day. On the business side, my grandparents can purchase a 50 pound bag of kernels from a restaurant supply store for around $20.00. Fifty pounds of kernels produces approximately 800 ounces of popped corn, for reference. Popcorn is sold in multiple sizes, but that 44 ounce bag tended to be a crowd favorite. While they still needed to purchase the popping oil, serving bags, salt, and butter topping, you can start to see how something as simple but well-loved as popcorn can make a great choice for your food truck.

Another more recent take on the food truck model is the incorporation of local dishes and ingredients. Often, this model hits the sweet spot between passion, skill, and cost. The menu for these types of food trucks includes mainly or exclusively locally-sourced products. If a food truck vendor and a local food producer decide to join forces, it's an opportunity for some magic to happen.

Though I try my best to explain to individuals from other states that Ohio is more than "just farms," there is, in fact, a lot of farmland to be found between Cleveland and Columbus, and Columbus and Cincinnati. The abundance of farmland translates into an impressive array of fresh produce, meats, cheeses, herbs, spices, and local honey.

This, in turn, gives locals the opportunity to join forces with a farm-to-table food truck model. In numerous locations, seasonal festivals will center around a particular crop's harvest or the production of a particular staple, such as the Circleville Pumpkin Festival, the Millersport Sweet Corn Festival, the Bucyrus Bratwurst Festival, the Geauga County Maple Festival, and a bevy of berry festivals around the state. Each of these festivals includes local food vendors who incorporate the celebrated product into their offerings.

Of course, these types of festivals and celebrations of local flavors are not exclusive to Ohio, and there may be many similar opportunities in your area. These relationships are often not limited to one type of food and can be mutually beneficial.

For example, a local pig farmer supplies pork to a local barbeque establishment at a reduced cost. The farmer can advertise that the truck sells his organically raised pigs, which gives the truck an advantage over other barbeque joints, while the truck can proudly announce that it is supplied by the farmer's business, which also sells to individuals at market prices. Again, the word "opportunity" appears, as both the local provider and the food truck vendor have the opportunity to share something special with the public as well as the opportunity to profit.

To summarize, there are a few very important questions you should ask yourself when deciding what you will sell from your food truck:

1. What do you love?
2. What can you make?
3. What will people buy?
4. What will it cost?

The ideal food truck menu will hit a sweet spot between all of these factors. Let's review these concepts using the examples I've introduced.

Linda loves dosa and knows what's needed to make and serve them. She also lives in an area where she is the only dosa operation. By limiting her menu to a few staples and engaging her husband's South Indian family in her business, she is able to easily produce and sell delicious products to an eager crowd.

My aunt enjoys baking delicious cheesecakes. In fact, she's gained a reputation for her cheesecakes. There is not a large selection of cheesecake vendors in her area, so when she adapted her cheesecakes to a traveling format, people were willing to pay for them.

My grandparents love providing hospitality and feeding as many hungry festival-goers as possible. They have chosen to sell very popular foods at a profitable price point. The foods they've chosen to sell can be purchased in bulk and stored, which means minimal waste. Plus, people will always have an appetite for simple items.

Then there's the symbiotic relationship between the pig farmer and the barbeque joint. Combining quality ingredients with amazing cooking techniques has resulted in both establishments gaining a very positive reputation, which means more business for each. Lower cost, higher quality ingredients means that the food truck vendor can invest in high quality ingredients beyond just the pork. The overall reputation and caliber of everything the truck has to offer means the owner can charge higher prices for his products. Meanwhile, the farmer relishes the new customer base, who want to try his product in their own recipes at home.

Choosing Your Menu

You may still feel a little indecisive about your menu. After all, even with a particular focus like dosa or cheesecake, there is a full range of options involved. I recommend starting with the vaguest, broadest concept possible, then narrowing it down step by step. This may require a little reworking or revisiting as your business plan comes to fruition, but you need to start with a concept in order to get that plan in motion.

For this exercise, I'm going to choose a pretty common, relatively straight-forward food concept: The taco truck. Nearly everyone has sampled a taco in their lifetime, and a taco truck includes a variety of options and ingredients to help illustrate the point of making these hard decisions in order to narrow down your plans.

So, we're going to build a taco truck. What do we need to make tacos? Generally speaking, we need meat, cheese, vegetables, and some kind of sauce, maybe a couple different types of sauce. But how do we decide which meat, cheese, vegetables, and sauce to choose?

Remember the sweet spot between passion, ability, sellability, and cost. Choose ingredients that are important to you, that you can easily prepare, that people want to eat, and that you will be able to afford. You might want to create a spreadsheet to help you scratch out some possibilities here.

One option is to create a multi-level spreadsheet to capture as much detail about each potential dish as possible. In the example I've provided, I brainstormed each dish by important notes, benefits, and challenges associated with that dish, along with the exact ingredients I'd put in the dish. I then calculated the "per serving" cost of each ingredient.

Jotting down all of the notes about each dish, including pros and cons, will help me decide if adding this dish to my menu is a good idea or not. If there are too many negative notes, such as "difficult to prepare", I might choose to leave that dish off the menu. Keep your notes, however. You might want to offer that dish as a special plate or even add it to the menu in the future if it really takes off.

Writing down all of the ingredients you intend to put in each dish can help in several different ways. First, you'll see how much you're putting in each serving of each dish, including both your ingredients and your money. Second, you'll be able to visually streamline your menu. Variety is the spice of life, but if you're serving five different tacos, all with different ingredients, you're going to need much more space to store and prep, a longer amount of time to prepare each order, and your overall food budget will be significantly higher. The more you use one ingredient, however, the more you can buy at a time. Bulk prices almost always offer savings. This will also bring down food waste, because you'll be using a significant amount of these items throughout each gig.

To put this into an example, let's say you have a taco that requires cucumber. Each taco requires just 1/10th of a cucumber, just a few slices. Cucumbers aren't terribly expensive in many markets, often around 50 cents. But each night, you only serve a handful of these tacos. Cucumber isn't known for staying fresh for long, which means that you're wasting a lot of cucumber. Despite costing "only" 50 cents, if you go through 4 cucumbers a week and sell the equivalent of 1 cucumber, you're just throwing money away.

Some people might feel that $2 per week is a fine amount to waste. $2 per week turns into $8 a month, or $104 a year. If you feel comfortable wasting $104 a year, that's certainly your prerogative, but that $104 could also go towards many other ingredients, upkeep of your vehicle, or paying your employees.

On the other hand, you put tomatoes on all of your tacos. Every taco gets about a fourth of a tomato on it. You sell one hundred tacos at a gig. Even though tomatoes cost more than cucumbers, you won't lose as much money on tomatoes. They store for a much longer period than cucumbers, and you can portion your tomatoes as strictly or judiciously as you need to adjust to the customer volume.

A chart such as the one below will help illustrate many key points about each menu item and ingredient, so I highly recommend creating these for every potential dish. I also encourage you to dream big and save your work. Even though that cucumber-topped taco doesn't make sense on paper now, it's time may come.

Taco #1	Notes	Ingredients	Cost	Per Taco (1oz per taco)
Ground Beef	Very popular	Soft taco shells 4 inch size	- $12/12	$1
	Possible to source grass-fed beef at a low cost from Henry's farm	Queso blanco	- $6 per half pound	$0.50
	Can use my famous seasoning mix for flavor	Lettuce	- $0.79 per head	$0.06
	Can prep ingredients ahead of time	Tomatoes	- $1 per lb	$0.08
	Can cook to order	Seasoning mix - my own blend	- $20 per lb	$1.25
	Meat must be stored carefully/ can't buy in huge bulk	Tortilla Chips	- $1.99 for 12 servings	$0.16
	Easy to serve and eat on the run	Meat	- $4 per lb	$0.25
		Total Cost Per Taco		Approx $3.30 per taco

Taco #1	Notes	Ingredients	Cost	Per Taco (1oz per taco)
– Chicken	– Lower fat meat source	– Soft taco shells 4inch size	– $12/12	– $1
	– Very popular	– Salsa	– $15 per gallon	– $0.11
	– Use salsa instead of cheese to keep cost down	– Lettuce	– $0.79 per head	– $0.06
	– No local source	– Tomatoes	– $1 per lb	– $0.08
	– Salmonella risks mean careful prep and storage	– Seasoning mix– my own blend	– $20 per lb	– $1.25
	– Hard to prep ahead of time, must cook on demand	– Tortilla Chips	– $1.99 for 12 servings	– $0.16
	– More expensive meat	– Meat	– $8 per lb	– $0.50
		– Total		– Approx $3.16 per taco

Please note: The prices in these examples are based on Columbus, Ohio market prices, so what you find on the shelves of your local market may be very different. I borrowed this recipe from a friend of mine who owns a taco restaurant. She buys her spices in bulk because she mixes them in bulk. If you are buying smaller quantities of spices, you might find that your costs vary.

As you can see, this chart provides a lot of information about two taco options. Based on this information, I would likely feel that both beef and chicken are pretty good options all around. They're both popular, they have a similar cost, and I can streamline a lot of the ingredients. There are a few negative points for each, mostly involving food storage, but this is to be expected. There will be plenty of challenges regardless of what you serve.

Once you have completed this exercise many times, you'll start to get a feel for what will and what won't work with your proposed food truck model. This might take some time. You may change your mind repeatedly based on your own preferences, the overall cost of ingredients, or for the sake of simplifying and streamlining. Don't be afraid to play with different options. Run your ideas past your friends or family. Try making the dishes for yourself and others. Test runs are always a good thing, because you'll gain more insight into a dish the more you prepare it.

After awhile, you will have a menu you feel pretty good about; in fact, you might feel downright triumphant. This is one of the most treasured moments in the process of creating your own food truck empire because suddenly the vision is clear. You can start to see the bigger pieces falling into place. You can almost see the outline of your truck on the horizon. Your dream is now officially on paper.

A Word About Beverages

In the food service world, hospitality is key. You want to provide your customers with the ultimate dining experience. There's a certain amount of etiquette and friendliness involved in making food service customers feel like valued guests instead of simply people making a business transaction.

As a result, many of us want to bend over backwards to make our customers happy. We want to provide them with food they will enjoy as well as enhance their dining experience. This remains true even when operating a food truck. You want people to have a glowing opinion of your operation.

But there are going to be some instances in which operating a food truck means you can't provide the comprehensive experience you would like to offer. One of these situations involves selling beverages.

Having a refreshing liquid to wash down a meal is pretty much a requirement of the human body, but can be difficult to facilitate in a food truck. In a small, deliberately designed space, less is usually more. Offering drinks of any kind means having to haul around more stuff, at the bare minimum, and can greatly increase your overhead very quickly.

Your two basic options for offering beverages are installing and operating a fountain drink dispenser, or selling bottles and cans. There are benefits and challenges with each option.

Fountain drinks may seem less expensive at first, but let's dive a little deeper. You'll need to either rent or buy a fountain dispenser from a restaurant supply store. That means your truck or trailer will need to have the following:

- Water filtration system
- Ice machine or ice storage/freezer
- A generator sufficient to power the fountain and the ice machine or freezer
- Room to store BIBs (Bag In Box - the method in which the soda syrup is stored and dispensed)

If you plan to purchase the fountain machine, you will need to learn how to service it yourself. These dispensers are notorious for clogging, and the plastic tubing that feeds the syrup to the machine can be temperamental in hot or cold weather. You'll have to take it apart for cleaning each time it is used to prevent the sugary syrup from clogging the machine.

On the other hand, if you rent the machine, you'll need to contact a preferred technician whenever something goes awry or risk voiding your rental contract.

You will also need to serve the drinks to your customers, which means adding the following items to your inventory:

- Cups - you will need to choose whether you sell one size, or multiple, and what type of cup, eg. styrofoam, paper, light plastic, etc.
- Lids
- Straws

Storing the BIBs might be the least onerous aspect of having them on board. Each one has approximately a two-month shelf life, even if you don't open them. They are also very heavy, and changing one requires opening the machine and sliding the used BIB out and the new one in while disconnecting and reconnecting the hosing without causing a giant mess. It's not impossible, I've done it many times by myself, but it does require a bit of technique to avoid creating a big, sticky, sugary puddle. Sure, the low cost of BIBs makes them seem ideal, but imagine trying to maneuver around a puddle of soda syrup in a tiny trailer in 90 degree heat, running a fryer and dodging bees. It is, in a word, miserable.

But it's not impossible, of course. While my Pawpaw spent equal time cursing the fountain machine and fixing it, the draw is undeniable. Hot fair goers love a giant fountain beverage, and the cost of a BIB is very low compared to what people are willing to pay for a 32 ounce ice-cold beverage.

The other option, and one that many food truck vendors prefer, is to sell beverages in cans and bottles. Buying cans and bottles will be much more expensive than buying a BIB. However, there are a significant amount of benefits to cans and bottles, such as:

- Long shelf life
- Minimal refrigeration required (no ice, no freezer - you can honestly just throw a bunch in a cooler for each gig)
- No maintenance, no equipment, no machinery

The types of beverages you sell opens up significantly here, as well. Rather than being limited to the types of BIBs you can source, or the branding on your machine (such as Coke or Pepsi products), you can sell anything you're able to make a profit on. Some food trucks that sell ethnic cuisine, for example, sell beverages that originate in the same region as the food. This creates the full dining experience without requiring a lot of effort or money.

Before you purchase your top ten beverages, however, remember that you will need to find a place to store cans and bottles between purchasing them and selling them at venues. Since they don't require refrigeration and have a longer shelf life than BIBs, you can easily tuck them into a corner of your garage or the truck/trailer when it's not in use instead of finding massive amounts of storage space, like you would need for BIBs.

You may be concerned that you'll run out of drinks if you buy a specific number of cans or bottles. There is a popular saying in the mobile food-service industry: "When you're out, you're out." I skimmed over this earlier when discussing my grandparents' hot dog truck, but the general idea is that if you run out of something it can be difficult to replace on the fly. There are a few exceptions, such as hot dogs. You can buy them anywhere, as long as you don't advertise a specific brand. As long as you have the time and a spare staff member you can buy hot dogs and cans of soda in any town in America. Otherwise, "when you're out, you're out!"

This logic also applies to drinks. But before you panic, think about the types of gigs you might be doing. Breweries and the like definitely have plenty to drink on hand. If you appear at a corporate office during lunch break, there's most likely a pop machine or water fountain inside. If you're at a fair or festival, there will be other trucks around - some of which will exclusively sell liquids, like the lemon shake-up stand, or the beer truck. Sure, it's no fun to lose business to a competitor, but between running out to get another case of diet root beer during a major rush and explaining to a guest that you are all out of diet root beer, but would they like a bottle of water, one choice is far more logical.

Another option for beverage service is coffee. Barista-style coffee vending is not a novice exercise. There are a lot of moving parts, and people are very specific about how they like their coffee. You'll also need to purchase and learn how to clean and service a commercial coffee maker, which is probably the easiest part. For simple drip coffee, you'll still need coffee and filters, as well as cream, sugar, sweeteners, thermal disposable cups with lids, and stir sticks. Coffee can be a great option for many food vendors. Just remember, people can be extremely fussy about their coffee, so either take your coffee as seriously as your customers or be sure to manage their expectations.

You'll also have to make sure coffee is constantly hot and fresh. Be very upfront about what you offer. If someone asked for a cup from my grandparents' trucks, we were instructed to say "yes sir/ma'am, we do have some coffee brewing back here. I can give you this size cup for a dollar. We only have powdered creamer, sugar, and the pink sweetener." That was fine for some people, and others would pass. Understand that everyone has feelings about coffee, and don't take their feedback personally.

An exception to all of these rules would be a beverage-specific business. For those of you who fall into this category, dealing in things like specialty coffee, lemon shake-ups, shaved ice, beer stands, etc., your primary focus at this stage should be figuring out what ingredients you need to make your beverages. Just like the taco examples, you can write out "cheat sheets" for each beverage you plan to sell. If you're running a coffee stand, for example, will you offer just cow's milk, or also non-dairy options like oat or almond milk? The same could be asked about a smoothie stand as well. When it comes to shaved ice, you'll need various flavored syrups, which might also be a consideration in a coffee stand if you plan to make flavored lattes and the like. Smoothies and shake ups require fruit, and ice is necessary all around.

Regardless of what type of mobile food business you have in mind, the steps outlined in this chapter will help you narrow down your options and help you make smart choices for your menu. First, decide what you want to sell. Then brainstorm your menu. Decide if you'll serve drinks and what types you plan to offer. Make notes throughout the process so you can remind yourself of why you chose to pursue or avoid a particular item or selection. There are so many moving pieces in the next several steps, that at some point, you might find yourself second-guessing your earlier decisions. Notes will help you stay on track.

Now that you have your menu in mind, you have your roadmap. From there, you'll be able to pick out your truck, and suddenly, you'll have a tangible home for the business of your dreams.

Chapter 2 How Will You Prep, Cook, and Serve Your Products?

Now that you've made plans for what will come out of your kitchen-on-wheels, you need to decide what you'll put inside your kitchen to make the so-called magic happen.

This is a spot in the process where some people choose to jump directly into buying their vehicle, be it a kitchen, truck, trailer, or cart. Once again, I would caution against doing this, as you might find yourself unable to build or install the equipment and fixtures you need in the truck that you choose. It's much easier to upfit a truck, trailer, or cart to your specifications than to find out that the space you've chosen won't work for your prep, storage, cooking, or serving needs.

Your kitchen setup depends on what you plan to serve. For the sake of continuity, I'll continue with the two tacos from the previous example throughout this exercise. Your own truck may look very different because you have very different needs, so keep that in mind as you read on.

If you're planning on running a restricted food truck business, which means all of your food is already prepared and pre-packaged, this part will be pretty straightforward, though you will have quite a few decisions to make. If you're serving hot food items, you'll need a temperature-regulated warmer that can keep everything hot without overheating or scorching your products. If you're interested in running an ice cream truck, you'll need a freezer that can run consistently cold enough to not melt your product. You'll need to worry less about different types of equipment, but you will need to pay attention to equipment size and specifications, to ensure you have the space and power for everything to function properly.

Let's start with the basics. Will your dishes be served hot, cold, or both? This will help you decide whether or not you need a grill or stove top, and if so, what size. For example, if you serve cold-cut sandwiches, smoothies, or cupcakes, you probably won't need a cook surface, so you can remove that from your list of needs altogether. If you're serving tacos, like in our example, you'll need a sizable cook surface where you can heat several orders of ground beef and chicken separately. If you're going to be serving the same dish with little variation, such as veggie burgers, you might be fine just having a smaller cook surface where you can keep a constant supply of that item heating during your business hours.

Hot Food Service Equipment

The most commonly found cooktop in a food truck is a griddle or flat top grill. This type of surface heats evenly all across the surface and is extremely versatile. You can use a flat top to grill meats, veggies, eggs, breads, and much more. If you've ever been to a grilled sandwich shop or Japanese steakhouse, this is the type of cooking surface you've likely encountered.

There are two basic types of flat top grill: electric and gas. Electric models have a heating element built into the griddle surface. These models generally heat slowly, but are very handy if gas or liquid propane are not practical for your truck or prohibited by local ordinances. Gas griddles have burners located under the griddle surface that are ignited by a pilot light (usually a button on the front of the griddle). These types of flat tops heat up very quickly but may require special ventilation systems, depending on local requirements.

From there, you have many different sizes and shapes to choose from. Small, portable countertop models are available, as well as "drop in" flat tops, which are permanently installed in a truck and connected to the main fixtures. Sizes can range from 12" to 72".

The plate of your flat top is very important, as well. Plate construction is typically stainless steel or chrome, and the preference is usually left to the chef, as both are very capable of cooking. There are three typical measurements of plates, which is the name for the actual cooking surface itself:

- Standard duty: 1/2" thick griddle plate
- Medium duty: 3/4" thick griddle plate
- Heavy duty: 1" thick griddle plate

These measurements can vary between manufacturers, so consider this a basic guideline and not a hard rule when shopping for your flat top. Thicker plates are associated with heavy-duty cooking, like turning a serving of frozen meat into an edible taco as quickly as possible. Thinner plates are best suited for ready-to-go foods, like eggs or vegetables, which generally require less time and heat to prepare.

A teppanyaki grill is another option. These grills tend to be larger in size, but only have heating elements in the center of the cooking surface. That means that the outer edges remain warm, which can be an excellent option for keeping prepared foods at the appropriate temperature while you're waiting to assemble and serve them to the customers.

You'll find plenty of differences between any two flat tops, so as you consider options, be sure to look at the type of base it has, as well as the specific controls. If you choose a countertop model, you'll definitely want a version that is very solid and stable. If you choose a drop-in, pay close attention to the size and the specifications for operation, such as the amount of electricity or type of gas required. You'll likely want a splash guard at the back to help contain any grease, oils, sauces, or ingredients that might get messy, and a trap drawer for collecting cooking debris in order to keep the cooking surface clean during use.

The other types of cooking equipment typically found in a food truck are probably far more familiar to you, such as toasters, microwave ovens, and range tops. A range top is what you encounter on a home stove, and much like the flat top, can be found in electric or gas versions, as well as larger drop-in models or smaller countertop versions. In fact, you can find single-burners, which might be ideal for a sauce or queso that needs to be kept warm throughout your serving hours.

Fryers present a series of special challenges when installed in a food truck; however, the popularity and profit margins on fried foods often make these challenges worth the effort. If you do not have an immediate or long-term need for a fryer, I strongly recommend choosing a small, portable or countertop model that you can quickly remove when it's not needed. Fryers can be either gas or electric-operated, and can range in size from countertop models to floor standing models, like you would expect to see at a busy fast food restaurant. They are generally measured by the number of gallons of oil they can hold, so be sure to check the overall specifications to get a feel for the vat size and overall footprint.

Here's the tricky part: operating a fryer requires large quantities of oil. Oil is somewhat of a fussy substance. If it gets too hot or is exposed to too much light, it will darken and taste bad. You'll need to change the oil frequently, and many mobile food vendors choose to filter it regularly to keep food tasting good and staying crispy. Filtration can involve options as low-tech as filter paper, to built-in filtration machines that cycle oil and remove food particles. Filtering oil can actually save a lot of money and frustration when compared to completely changing out the oil each time it starts to get dark.

Regardless of whether you choose to filter your oil or not, you will need to dump your used oil every few uses. The term is somewhat misleading, as you can't just dispose of it anywhere you like. For operations with a high volume of frying and oil, there are companies that will do all of the regular fryer maintenance for you. You pay for cleaning, service, and removal of older oil. This type of service might be out of scope if you are a smaller or newer food truck business. Another option is grease receptacles. If you have access to a grease receptacle, you'll simply empty the old fryer oil into a stock pot and dump it carefully into the bin. You may also be able to contract with someone who wants to recycle your used oil for fuel or other purposes. You'll need to investigate options in your area, but they will typically collect your used fuel at no or little cost to you.

Every time you do an oil change, you may wish to boil out your fryer to ensure it's completely clean. This process involves completely draining all of the oil, adding a heady mixture of deep fat cleanser and water, then bringing it to a boil to remove any residue in the fryer.

Fryers also tend to splatter grease enthusiastically, so you'll want to place a fryer far from other cooking surfaces or prep surfaces to avoid cross-contamination, or install dividers between the fryer and these areas.

The last element is keeping your hot foods hot. Ideally, you'll prepare an order and immediately hand it to a waiting guest. However, there are a few situations in which you might need to keep things warm.

The first is a fry dump station. Fried food can take a little time to prepare, and unless you advertise made-to-order products, it might speed up your wait time to prepare a large order of french fries, onion rings, or tortilla chips at once, and keep them in a fry dump, which is a piece of equipment that keeps fried food hot and crispy through a combination of warming lights and a base fitted with a grate, which prevents oil from pooling under the food as it waits.

You might also want to prepare some large-quantity items in bulk before a rush. For example, if you decide to serve fajita veggies on your tacos for an upcharge, you may wish to make those in bulk before a big rush, so that you can focus your cooking space on the ground beef and chicken. These are essentially electric chafing dishes, or *Bain-marie*, if you have food industry experience, which surround a dish full of cooked food with water, which can be temperature controlled to keep that food hot for longer periods of time. You've likely seen a version of these at buffets.
Heated display cases and soup stations are also options you might wish to pursue if you'll serve things like baked goods, soup, curries, or stews.

Elements of Refrigeration

With the exception of smaller food carts, refrigeration is key to nearly every food truck. From safely transporting ingredients and storing them at the correct temperature throughout the gig, to keeping bottles and cans of beverages chilled, most food trucks require a refrigerator.

The most popular option is the worktop or under-counter refrigerator. Just as the name implies, the refrigerator is stashed under your counter, or comes with a stainless steel worktop already installed. That way, the top of the unit can be used as a prep area, while still working hard to keep those key ingredients cold and fresh.

This is not to be confused with a preparation refrigerator. These models feature a top suitable for preparation, but also include a refrigerated cabinet section on top, where pans of pre-cut ingredients can be stored. Using our taco truck model, you could place pans of pre-diced tomatoes and pre-shredded lettuce in the hinged cabinet on top, so that you can easily grab them and throw them onto the tacos you're preparing, rather than having to bend over to retrieve toppings, or allowing them to sit too long on the countertops. Preparation refrigerators are most common when serving dishes that have several toppings or assembly options, such as sandwiches, salads, or pizzas.

As with all other equipment, you'll want to be sensible about the size of your refrigerator. You'll also want to make note of the temperature capabilities to ensure that you're able to keep things nicely chilled. Additionally, check the voltage. You don't want to overload your generator.

Then there's the ice machine. This is another piece of equipment, like the fryer or cooktop, that should only be installed if necessary due to the size and complexity of the equipment. Of course, if you're planning on serving smoothies or frozen coffee drinks, it's completely necessary. Luckily, smaller under-counter models are available so you don't have to sacrifice floor or prep space.

Ice makers require a power source and a water source. Since not all water sources are created to the same standards, you'll also want a water filtration device. Ice machines also may include air filters, and require frequent cleaning to ensure the ice you serve is safe, clean, and delicious.

When it comes to choosing an ice maker, take a look at the quantity and type of ice made. There are different sizes and shapes of ice cubes or chips, so make sure the model you purchase is able to provide what you need. Also, look at the footprint and shape. A sliding door will be far more practical than a door that swings open, so that you don't bang anyone in the kneecaps when fetching ice. One with adjustable legs will have better ventilation than one that rests directly on the floor of your truck. As a word of caution, you will want to make sure you retrieve anything that rolls under it immediately. Rodents and bugs are very tempted by the tasty things that fall under equipment!

Cooking Gear and Storage

One you have the major appliances planned, you'll need to take stock of the overall preparation process so you can decide what types of tools and utensils you need. Granted, this is the easiest stock element to change, as you can pick up pans and spatulas nearly any place, but the goal here is to give more consideration to all of the "stuff" that will be in your truck. Thinking about this now, as opposed to once business is booming, will help you be in the right headspace for some decisions you'll be making in the very near future -- big decisions like counter space versus storage space. It can even make the difference between your decision to buy a full-blown truck over a trailer. You'll also be writing out detailed prep notes for you and your staff to follow, which will require descriptions of every piece of equipment involved in each dish.

So, while you have all of your notes on potential dishes and equipment in front of you, start drafting the specific equipment you'll need to make everything happen. To get you started, here are just a few examples of things you might want to bring along from gig to gig:

- Specialty equipment, such as a blender, juicer, potato peeler, fry cutter, popcorn popper, hot dog turner, gyro spinner, toaster, or dough/tortilla press

- Storage containers for prepared items, such as steel or plastic bins
- Cutting boards
- Knives and safe knife storage
- Turners and spatulas
- Food thermometers
- Tongs, spoons, and strainers
- Sauce pans or skillets
- Shakers or squeeze bottles for toppings applied before serving
- Your point of sale (POS) system (which we'll discuss in more detail in the chapter regarding business decisions)

While you're thinking of these things, consider how you might like to store them while in transit. You'll have a clearer picture of opportunities once you actually start looking at trailers and trucks to call your own, but a general idea will help you pare down your list to what you actually need, as opposed to what you feel you ought to have on hand.

There are two very important things to remember about food trucks and storage:

1. They move. This means everything will move around in transit, and there will even be some shifting and settling once you're parked. If you have drawers, consider dividers to prevent utensils from tangling and getting damaged. You can't just set things down on a counter, because they'll slide all over the place once you hit the road. Even the things you put in the refrigerator will slosh around, unless they're strapped in or pinned down. Many food truck veterans have a healthy supply of adhesive Velcro, zip ties, and duct tape on hand to prevent calamity from things shifting. Magnetized strips can also be helpful for keeping utensils and small items readily grabbable by staff without getting lost in the fast-paced shuffle.
2. Space is at a premium. You might love the way a certain type of spiralizer looks, but if it takes up so much space that you can't fit a catch bucket under it for your spiral potatoes to drop into, it might not be the right fit for your truck or trailer. You need to strike a bal-

ance between compact, lightweight, and heavy duty when choosing all of the items that outfit your mobile food business. You'll want it to fit and function every time you need it, which means not having to clear off a specific space for it in the middle of a rush, and not dealing with frequent mechanical failure.

When making decisions about overhead cabinets, countertops, and under-counter storage, think of function first and foremost. You need something that will be easy to sanitize. You'll need to be able to open and close doors quickly without banging yourself and your staff in the head or knees. You don't want to construct a labyrinth of storage in your trailer or truck. Everything needs to be accessible.

For transportation storage, many food truck operators use heavy-duty storage bins that are waterproof and have handles for easy carrying. Although you can always use the same plastic bins that are storing your off-season clothing in the garage, it's much better to purposefully select the bins that fit your exact food truck needs. These can be picked up at any home improvement store. They come in all shapes and sizes and are surprisingly inexpensive for how essential they are. Storage bins are perfect for utensils, non-perishable ingredients, serveware, and all the loose odds and ends you need to bring with you. Keep your bins organized. It's a great idea to have a checklist for each bin to make sure everything gets to the gig and that everything comes home as well.

Of course, this is just a preliminary phase, in which you're brainstorming ideas. Later, once you've actually started looking at trucks and trailers, you'll have a more realistic picture of what will work, but having a general plan now will give you a head start, rather than scratching your head and attempting to make things fit as you head towards your first gig.

Serving Gear

The main goal of your serving gear is to get each and every one of your dishes from the inside of your truck, through a window, and safely into the hands of your guests. Gloves for the workers inside your truck is a given, but the packaging that your customers handle can look very different depending on what you're serving.

You'll want to think about the temperature of the food, as well as the overall potential for messiness. For example, your typical sandwich/wrap/burger/hot dog might need nothing more than a wax paper or foil wrapper, depending on whether it's served hot or cold. A taco, on the other hand, might benefit from a paper boat to catch all of the toppings that might drip out while the customer attempts to eat it.

My favorite example of balancing "hot" and "messy" is the funnel cake, because it is challenging from both perspectives. For those who have never tried one, a funnel cake is made of a prepared dough, which is poured through a funnel into a shallow fryer full of hot grease. It must be rapidly turned by hand during the frying process to avoid burning. Once it reaches a crispy gold on both sides, it is served with a hearty dusting of powdered sugar, a drizzle of hot fudge, or even as a sundae. Funnel cakes are generally made to order, because they get soggy quickly as they absorb the fryer oil residue.

The ideal plating for a funnel cake involves a surface that is larger than the cake itself, so no one burns their fingers trying to carry it, along with a barrier that prevents the grease from dripping, melting, or soaking through. My grandparents chose to serve their funnel cakes on a doubled-up pair of paper plates with a piece of food-service-grade foil on top. The foil prevented the grease from soaking through the paper plates, and the paper plates helped give the customer something to hold on to to carry their fried doughy goodness. Paper plates and foil: it can be that simple.

This concept goes for beverages, as well. If you're serving coffee drinks, you'll want to use cups that can handle very hot temperatures without burning hands. If you're serving frozen drinks, you'll need cups that won't crack or shatter when they get cold. You'll also want to consider lids, sleeves, and straws. Lastly, what sizes will you offer? While customers love a choice, you will have to store each different size of cup and each different size of lid somewhere in your food truck or trailer for the duration of each gig.

You'll also need to consider portion sizes, and attempt to consolidate items as much as possible. If you're serving a burger with fries, you may be tempted to wrap the burger in foil and shovel the fries into a cardboard cup. Depending on the type of gig, however, it might make more sense to use a larger styrofoam to-go box to house both the burger and fries, as it will be less for your customers to juggle when their family of four decides they each want their own meal!

Condiments are a huge area of debate, as mentioned earlier when reviewing coffee service. Not only will you have to decide which ones to serve, but how to serve them.

My first recommendation is to remember that you cannot predict how everyone will want to spice up their meals. While many people enjoy their french fries with catsup (or ketchup in some parts of the world), some prefer vinegar and salt, others like mayonnaise, ranch dressing, or even chocolate milkshakes. Unless each of these items has a practical application in your menu, there is no need to offer all of these. While you want your guests to have an enjoyable experience, you cannot offer them all of the flavors of your local market's condiment aisle at once.

Now, let's talk about condiments. I recommend picking a few staples. If you've ever purchased food at a large sports stadium, you'll be familiar with the large communal tubs of ketchup, mustard, stadium mustard, and individual packets of relish or mayonnaise.

Following the COVID-19 situation of 2020, you may not feel comfortable carrying around communal condiments, and these feelings are valid. You do have the option to offer packets of condiments appropriate to your dishes. You may also wish to purchase small condiment cups that you can hand out upon request. This option allows you to save money by purchasing the bulk containers, but keeps them under your control, which means fewer hands are touching them.

If you have a specialty condiment, such as a gourmet mayonnaise, chutney, or salsa, these small condiment cups are a saving grace. Offered with or without lids, they do incur expenses, but you don't have to worry about self-serve food waste. You can also charge accordingly for extra, instead of helplessly watching packets and cups being thrown into the waste bins around you.

You'll also want to consider utensils and napkins. For the sake of expenses, waste, and the planet, I recommend the minimum for your cuisine, though there will always be someone who wants a knife with their smoothie or a spoon with their french fries. You may wish to keep some disposable utensils on hand for such occasions, but if your dishes don't require them, don't offer them. Of course, you'll want to offer a soup spoon with soup, or a fork with pasta, but don't go overboard with providing too many options. Everything you put in your truck has a price tag and requires valuable space, so keep that in mind as you plan your shopping list.

Napkins are also a consideration for almost every food truck. You may wish to put out a serve-yourself napkin dispenser, or you may wish to provide each customer with one heavy-duty napkin. You may wish to do both. I recommend considering the consistency of your food and your venue when choosing what to offer. Lobster rolls at a brewery, for example, would be less concerning than pizza at a concert. The brewery likely has seating areas where folks can enjoy their meal, an easily accessed bathroom, and cocktail napkins available at the bar or service area.

Lastly, there's the question of what type of serveware to purchase. Disposable products are traditionally bad for the environment, though "green" options do exist. Styrofoam, waxed paper, and plastic will be less expensive than bio-friendly and post-recycled options, but I have to admit that seeing the grounds of a venue littered with those items after the crowds have gone home does drive home the point about waste and our environment. At the same time, it's impossible to expect fairgoers, concert attendees, and folks wandering out of a club at three A.M. to have their own reusable forks, plates, and straws on hand, so they are a necessary evil.

Bear in mind that the "when you're out, you're out" principle also extends to serving supplies. If you don't have the ability to wrap, box, bag, scoop, or otherwise place your food items in a container, you are no longer able to serve food, which means closing for the day. That means loss of revenue, and if you're not far into a gig (meaning, you have hours to go before you would normally have last call and start to strike for the night), you'll lose favor in the eyes of both the venue operator and your customers. If you are going to run out of anything, it should not be serving supplies. That means serving gear should be at the top of your list for taking inventory, as well as a major consideration in your storage plans.

Taking in this information, you may feel a little intimidated about what needs to be inside your food truck in order for your dreams to become a reality. At this point, you're just getting ideas, so don't worry about having to run out and buy all of these items right this second. Instead, make notes. Start organizing your ideas, and keep track of things that come to mind. Remember, not every food truck will need condiment packets. Spoons might be completely irrelevant to your service plan. Don't let yourself get overwhelmed by the number of options there are; instead, focus on the ideas that work best for you.

Chapter 3 Food Truck Biomechanics

The inside of a food truck is essentially a very small commercial kitchen. Those who have worked in fast food restaurants, large commercial kitchens, and fine dining establishments might find the close quarters hard to get accustomed to, but those who have worked on deli lines or low-volume restaurants will be able to appreciate the layout right away.

Most food trucks have a lateral layout due to the size and shape of the space. This means work spaces on both of the long sides of the vehicle or trailer, with an aisle in the middle. A service window will generally take up the upper half of one side, which means that space will not be available for cabinets or fixtures.

So, where do you put everything? And what are your absolute requirements for your space? Let's look at some of the basic physical needs of your food truck or trailer before you start shopping for your vehicle. This way, you'll feel better prepared to evaluate whether or not that space will meet your needs. Can it work with some remodeling and refitting, or will it simply not work at all? Remember, there's no "universal fit" for a food truck.

Getting It Together: Prep Space and Sinks

When it comes to preparation of your dishes, step back and think step by step about how a particular ingredient goes from the state in which you purchased it to becoming a feature in your dishes.

For example:

Tomatoes for Tacos
1. Purchase fresh tomatoes
2. Wash thoroughly
3. Chop into cubes
4. Prepare 1 ounce of tomato per taco

Now consider how much time it would take to chop 1 ounce of tomato per taco each time one is ordered. While that's definitely something you could do on the fly, making a regular habit of it will drive up your food wait times incredibly.

Instead, wouldn't it make more sense to chop all of the tomato ahead of time? You could chop loads of tomato, keep it all in a prep bin, and tuck it in the refrigerator with a lid or cling wrap protecting it until it's "go time."

Do this for all of your ingredients to determine if they should show up at the venue with you ready to go, or if you'll need to prepare them fresh.

One thing you might prefer to prepare fresh is your meat products. Let's use the same step-by-step chart to review how that would work:

Ground Beef for Tacos
1. Henry drops off an order of fresh ground beef
2. Weigh and portion out 1-ounce servings
3. Season with special seasoning
4. Chill for an hour minimum to let the seasoning "set"
5. Place on a grill and cook until brown
6. Add salsa
7. Serve on a taco

In this case, you also have an opportunity to get some of the prep work out of the way before you show up at a gig: You can portion out and season the raw meat ahead of time. These portions can even be frozen for future use. Remember that raw meat has a very short shelf life, but frozen meat can last a few months. Pre-portioning and seasoning ahead of time gives you the opportunity to grab and cook one portion at a time once the orders start rolling in.

Just a word of caution- if you do decide to freeze pre-portioned meat, make sure you have plenty of time for it to thaw correctly in a refrigerator before your gig. While some cook surfaces are great at bringing products from frozen to edible, it will take extra time while your hungry customers will be waiting.

One general rule is that the prep space in your food truck should be for the last stages of prep, not for the whole process. In fact, most mobile food vendors, from the smallest food cart to the biggest mobile kitchen, do the real prep-work off site. We'll explore this topic more shortly. Many vendors take advantage of commissaries or open restaurant space to take care of the more labor-intensive parts of preparation, leaving the space in the truck for cooking and assembling.

On the other hand, you might not have a lot to prep, depending on the choices you've made. In an elephant ear and funnel cake stand, you simply need to measure and dump the necessary amount of powdered dough mix and water in a stand mixer, mix until smooth, and portion it out. Popcorn prep involves putting corn and oil in the popcorn machine. Hot dogs involve pulling them out of the packet and securing them in the roaster. These types of trucks specifically require the least amount of prep, which means the trailer can be designed with very little counter space.

As I've said many times, food trucks and trailers are not "one size fits all." Don't feel you need 48" of pristine stainless steel counter space with a built in cutting surface just because you saw that on television. If a prep fridge with a hatchback storage area makes sense for your business model, plan for one. If you only need a refrigerator for beverages, you might simply place a cooler of drinks just outside the door.

One element that every food truck or trailer needs, not just for prep, but for overall food safety, is a sink. In most cases, state or local food service guidelines require a sink. Always check with your area's requirements first, but generally speaking, a three compartment sink and hand washing sink with hot water are required for any establishment serving food to the public. Some states even specifically forbid handwashing in the dish sink, so pay close attention to these requirements.

Additional requirements may indicate that your waste water tank needs to be a certain amount larger than your clean water tank (usually 15%) and that your sink is large enough to adequately fit and sanitize your largest piece of equipment. You'll also need to ensure your water can heat to a specific temperature (usually 180 degrees Fahrenheit).

Therefore, in addition to four sink compartments, you will also need a fresh water supply, a waste water tank, and a heating element in order for your food truck to pass the health code.

There are a few ways to accommodate these requirements, but not all are approved by the Food and Drug Administration or your local health department. I cannot stress enough that you will need to check your local regulations before you finalize your food truck. There will be more information about all the legal steps in the next section and links in the Resources section to help guide you through this.

Some food trucks have a water supply that works with the help of gravity. The freshwater tank is stashed above the sink, either on the wall or ceiling, and the laws of physics help deliver water through the piping and faucet. A water pump is another way to create water flow on demand. This pump is powered by your generator, so you'll want to be diligent about the generator's capacity. Any freshwater tank must be cleaned and sterilized frequently, because standing water is a haven for bacteria growth. Single-piece polyethylene plaster resin is the most popular choice for water tanks, as they are made of food-safe materials, do not have seams that can crack or leak, and are non-corrosive.

Hot water can be achieved by adding a water heater to your set up. You can choose electric or gas/propane, but bear in mind that both have their own requirements. Electric models must fit within the guidelines of your generator, and gas needs its own ventilation system. We'll talk more about various ventilation systems next.

The three compartments of the sink are designated for different steps in the washing/sanitizing process. Though washing dishes and prep materials in a food truck is highly regulated, don't be intimidated. The process is just like what you do at home, only with specific step and temperature requirements. You're just incorporating some extra details into what you usually do.

First, you'll need a process for removal and disposal of big chunks of stuck-on food. Then it's time to wash. The first compartment of the sink is designated for washing with an approved detergent. The water should be a minimum of 110 degrees Fahrenheit. The second compartment is then for rinsing the detergent from the dishes. The third compartment of the sink is for sanitation. Many mobile food vendors use a chemical sanitizer and hot water, since that requires the least effort and attention. In most cases, you can submerge the dishes and work on something else while they sanitize, but always follow the directions on the sanitizer to the letter. Finally, washed, rinsed, and sanitized dishes should be allowed to air dry, either on a drip drying rack above the sink or a drainboard to the side.

Your handwashing sink can be much smaller than your dishwashing sink, but will need to provide hot water for frequent handwashing.

As mentioned earlier, you'll want your "grey" water, or wastewater, tank to have a greater capacity than your freshwater. This tank isn't just accommodating used water, but also any waste or grease that is rinsed off of your dishes as they are cleaned, and potentially any liquids or beverages that are poured down the drain through the course of your serving gig. Grey water tanks can be installed under the truck itself or under the sink to keep them out of the way while you're in business.

Some state health departments have requirements as to how much fresh and grey water storage must be available at all times. I fully encourage you to look this up at this stage of the process so there are no surprises after you've purchased your food truck or trailer. Remember that one gallon of water weighs approximately 8 pounds, which will be calculated into your weight and hauling capacity, as well.

Making It All Work: Ventilation, Generators, and Fuel

The last integral part of your food truck set up will be ventilation, fuel sources, and generators. I wish it were as simple as saying, "Alright, so you need one ventilator hood in this size, two XX-gallon propane tanks, and a such-and-such generator." Naturally, it's a lot more involved than that, so let's instead look at the purpose and needs for each piece of equipment so you are prepared to shop for a truck that either already has these installed or can be fitted with the equipment you need.

Mechanical ventilation in your food truck or concession trailer is a great idea for many reasons. First of all, bodies moving around in a small, enclosed area will require additional air circulation. Then take into consideration the cooking and the equipment. Imagine how warm you get cooking a simple meal in your home kitchen. Now imagine doing that for several hours straight. Steam, smoke, and tiny airborne grease particles will continue to build up in your enclosed food truck as you prep, cook, and serve. When your surfaces get coated with tiny grease particles and moisture, you'll get a filmy, greasy build up, which can corrode surfaces over time.

Just like everything else in a mobile food operation, the requirements for ventilation vary from location to location. Some states require open, unobstructed windows or doors during operation, while others require a ventilation hood for every part of cooking equipment, including the grill top, fryers, charbroilers, etc. Some require integrated fire suppression systems like sprinkler systems. There may be requirements for the distance between ventilation components and other items within your food truck.

Ventilation systems for food trucks typically exhaust from the top of the structure or through an exterior wall. You've likely seen the mushroom-shaped exhaust feature on a truck before and wondered exactly what it does.

Inside, you'll want to install exhaust hoods specific to the equipment they are intended to ventilate. Type I exhaust hoods are used for grease-producing cooking equipment such as fryers, and Type II exhaust hoods are for cooking elements that do not use grease, such as ovens.

The next consideration for your cooking equipment is power generation.

Diesel and gas-powered generators are the most popular component for powering food trucks. They are relatively inexpensive to own and operate, have a long lifespan, and produce a consistent flow of power for long stretches of time. On the other hand, they are noisy and produce noxious fumes in addition to the delicious food smells emanating from your truck.

When considering a generator for your food truck, look at size, capability, and, of course, your local emissions requirements. Look at the dimensions and the weight of each generator. It will need to travel with you, and while very small generators are available, they may not provide enough power to operate all of the necessary appliances. Additionally, generators require sufficient ventilation to cool them and allow carbon monoxide output to dissipate safely, so unlike a water tank, it can't be tucked away somewhere unseen.

You'll also need to make sure the output of the generator is correct for your equipment. This involves paying attention to the wattage, voltage, and amperes (or amps). If you have a background in electrical engineering, this part will make perfect sense. If you have only a passing familiarity with the concept that power out and power in must be compatible or things get sparky and smoky, you're likely a little lost. Don't worry, you're not alone.

Most food trucks can safely operate with a 5,000-7,000 watt generator. If you have a lot of appliances, lights, fans, and one of those flailing tube advertising gimmicks running at once, you might want to step up to a 10,000 watt model. For your truck, you'll need to know the starting wattage and running wattage of your appliances. Some appliances, like refrigerators, are known as "reactive loads," which means they require a lot of power to start up but not a lot of power to run. Other appliances are "resistive loads," and require the same amount of power from the moment you plug it in to the moment you unplug it. A light bulb is a good example of a resistive load.

To calculate the overall wattage you'll need, you must add up the individual wattage of each appliance that will be running at once. For reactive loads, use the starting wattage to prevent overloading your generator.

If reading this is making your head swim, stay calm. There are some very particular mechanical operations involved with operating a food truck; however, you do not have to be a specialist in all of these areas. Just as you may not change the oil and rotate the tires on your own vehicle, you don't have to rush out and get an electrician's certification to operate your food truck. What you do need is the ability to find and make note of the wattage of all of your appliances and your generator. You may wish to involve a professional who can help you understand the specific needs of your generator. You will need to understand basic operation and maintenance issues that may arise and when to call for professional assistance.

You'll find several resources for videos regarding generators in the Resources section. I encourage you to learn the basics, just as you have learned basic upkeep of your car, your home, your pets, and yourself.

If a gas powered generator sounds completely unappealing, I will note that there have been recent advancements in solar powering food trucks. This is the more environmentally conscious choice and requires very little upkeep after installation. Solar panels don't require fuel and make absolutely no noise. However, they can be very pricey to install, and you may need a full array of panels to provide enough electricity for all of your truck's components. They're also dependent upon sunlight and good weather, which might be a challenge depending on your location.

As for your gas-powered cooking appliances, you'll need to bring along your own supply. This means bringing along propane tanks, and having your food truck outfitted with a propane system. I highly encourage leaving this process to the professionals, because of all of the extremely combustible moving pieces involved. There are pipes traveling from the tanks to the appliances, pressure valves, regulators, and everything is very flammable.

Far simpler is determining what size tank you need. Each appliance that requires propane will have a BTU (British Thermal Unit) rating in the owner's manual. Add up each BTU rating for all appliances that will be running simultaneously, then divide the BTU capacity of your propane tank by the total BTU requirements to determine how many hours you can get out of each tank.

For reference:

- 20 lb. propane tank has a 430,270 BTU capacity
- 30 lb. propane tank has a 649,980 BTU capacity
- 40 lb. propane tank has a 860,542 BTU capacity
- 100 lb. propane tank has a 2,160,509 BTU capacity

You may require several propane tanks per gig. Remember to store these safely, check for leaks frequently, never use damaged, dented, or rusty tanks, and always exercise caution around equipment that requires fuel for operation.

When looking at ventilation, generators, and fuel for your food truck, I recommend erring on the side of safety in every possible way. The National Fire Prevention Association has some great tips for food truck operations when it comes to fuel storage and commercial cooking operations. You'll find these links and more in the Resources section.

In Summary

We have covered a LOT of ground in this section, and all of it is equally important. On one hand, your head might be swimming with facts and figures and ideas and concepts. On the other hand, you are now armed with all of the information you need to create your business plan, buy your food truck, and start stocking it in preparation for your first gig, which we will cover in the next section.

To summarize all of the information that we've discussed in this chapter, I've created a handy cheat sheet to help you organize these thoughts into usable notes going forward. Below are the concepts and main thoughts covered in each part of this section.

Food Truck Requirement	Key Points
Serving Food	Create a balance between food you love, your ability to cook, cost, and potential profit
Serving Beverages	Fountain drinks may be less expensive, but require greater maintenance and more supplies. Is it practical or necessary to serve beverages at all?
Heating and Keeping Food Hot	Consider if you'll want to install a flat top grill, fryers, ovens, burners, or other equipment. You may also consider heat lamps, Bain-maries, and heating cases.

Refrigeration	Under counter refrigerators and prep fridge stations are both popular in food trucks. If you require ice, you will need to consider an ice maker.
Supplies and Storage for Everything	You must decide how to balance the equipment you need with the space available. Equipment must be secured during travel.
Serving Supplies	Wrappers or containers must be provided for all food items. You may also wish to provide utensils, condiments, and napkins. Drinks will require cups, and you may wish to offer lids and straws.
Preparation Space	Consider using your food truck for the final stages of preparation, rather than all steps.
Sinks	You will need a three-compartment sink for washing, rinsing, and sanitizing. You will need a separate hand washing sink.
Water	You must bring along fresh water and grey water storage tanks. Non-corrosive food safe tanks are recommended. You must also have a water heater for dishwashing and handwashing.
Ventilation	As required by regulations. Can help remove smoke, grease, and steam, as well as improve air flow.
Gas-Powered Generator	Consider the physical size and wattage. Safety first.
Fuel/Propane Tank	Determine the size required for the appliances connected. Consult with a professional. Exercise caution.

Section 3 The Business of Making Dreams Come True : Forming Plans and Buying Pans

It's time to start making actual plans. While the last section included a lot of brainstorming about physical, tangible things, like whether you'll need a fryer and what type of sink you'll need, this section will feature a lot of administrative things, like securing finances and permits, or nailing down procedures. You will get to do some exciting things as well, like shopping for your own food truck and getting everything ready for your business to take off.

While administrative "stuff" usually doesn't rate as many people's idea of a good time, it is necessary when establishing a business. We'll start with your business plan, financing, and the legal requirements. Once you have a solid idea of where you want to be, we'll figure out how to get your business on the road, starting with your truck and home base, and then filling it with supplies, staff, procedures, and all of your hopes and dreams.

Chapter 1 Creating a Business Plan

If your first reaction to the title of this chapter was "do I really have to?" you're not alone. Creating a business plan is tedious, requires a lot of thought, and can make you question whether you really want to follow through with your dreams.

At the same time, a business plan will be required to convince your investors that you're creating a well-thought-out plan, which makes them more willing to hand over their hard-earned money. Even if you don't require financial assistance, writing a business plan will help keep all of your thoughts and ideas organized.

Your business plan can be as informal or as detailed as you (or your investors) would like it to be, but there are a few elements that should be included.

First, I recommend jotting down an Executive Summary. That sounds super fancy, but it essentially boils down to the "why, where, who, what, and how" of your proposed mobile food business. Why does your business need to exist? Where are you operating? Who is your target market? What is the purpose of your business? How do you plan to differentiate your business within the local market?

The next sections of the business plan will provide additional support and justification for your business. If you are creating this plan to streamline your own ideas, you may not need to get into a significant amount of detail, but many investors will want you to "show your work," so to demonstrate why your food truck is a good use of their money. This includes identifying a need for your food truck, and pointing out key factors that can determine your success: Who are your competitors? Who is your target audience? Why are *you* uniquely prepared to succeed in this business?

Your plan will include a basic outline of your operation: How often do you plan to take your truck out? What type of staff do you plan to hire? How many units do you hope to serve each week/month/year? How will you measure success or failure?

If you are using this business plan to secure financial backing, you will also want to provide your own financial forecast. It's important that you base this on actual facts and figures. This includes all monthly costs, such as food costs, maintenance, operations, marketing, staffing, and travel, as well as what you anticipate for profits. Obviously, you will not be able to predict this with great accuracy; however, you can include data on how often you plan to book gigs, what you plan to charge for each menu item, which will then help you create monthly targets to recoup your expenses. Any financer will need to be convinced that you have done your homework.

This may require some reconnaissance, such as researching the average cost of various ingredients or the wages of staff in your area, and comparing what other food trucks and restaurants in your area charge for similar dishes. It's hard to describe how frustrating creating these financial forecasts can be, especially since you may not have the funding at this stage to actually secure vendors, and the overall market and economy in your area can change on a whim. Still, keep calm and know that this is intended not to be the crystal ball to your future, but to project your goals based on the market and costs that currently exist.

More detail may be required for investors, including a three-year projection, tax considerations, insurance provisions, a statement of your current equity, and an overall risk assessment for projected expenses. This means more research on your behalf, along with more math, and even worse, having to dream of potential disasters so you can be financially prepared for them. You may even be asked to provide appraisals of resale value on used equipment if things don't work out in your favor.

You may wish to evaluate these figures even if you aren't looking for financial assistance. Knowing the value of what you have against its replacement value, versus what you would get for selling it is a great equation for determining the value for every item you purchase going forward. You will be tempted at many points to get the "newest and shiniest," but in many cases, the best practice for any business is to invest in the best overall value.

Finding the Money

When it comes to starting a business, no step is more of a reality check than looking at the financials.

I've compiled a chart of all of the basic expense groups for the typical mobile food business. Your state may require certain inspections and your locality might require others. You may have to apply for a variety of specific permits, depending on where you plan to operate your business. If you purchase a food truck, as in a vehicle with its own motor, you won't need a truck like you would if you purchased a trailer, or even a pushcart.

This is a chart that you will visit over and over again. Each time you need to evaluate a vendor, a replacement, or an upgrade, review this chart to determine how the expense fits into your overall financial plan.

This chart doesn't include emergencies. What you tuck away for emergencies will depend on your insurance deductible and any liabilities included in the various contracts you sign for each gig.

With this in mind, take a look at this chart, and for each section in the left column, consider what you might anticipate as expenses based on your research so far.

Food truck, trailer, pushcart

Insurance

Inspection Fees (health inspection, OSHA, etc.) and Code Prep

Business License, Taxes, etc.

Generator, Propane, Water (maintenance and supplies)

Appliances (Grill, fryer, refrigerator, ice maker, sinks, water heater, toaster, blender, fry dump, etc.)

Equipment: pans, turners, spatulas, prep containers, specialty pieces, foil, cling wrap, fire extinguisher, etc.

Service gear and paper goods: wrappers, napkins, containers, cups, lids, condiments, condiment cups, stir sticks, utensils, straws, etc.

Staff required gear: gloves, hair nets/hats, aprons

Point of sale system (tablet or register)

Cleaning Supplies: dishwashing soap, dish sanitizer, broom, mop, bucket, hand washing soap, clean clothes and towels

Labor/Staffing

Food: All ingredients, portioned per recipes

Drinks

Signage/ Marketing

Other optional considerations: Commissary, vehicle to pull the trailer, contractor to upfit or remodel, storage facility

As you work on this exercise, pull real figures from the research you have done along the way, or enter estimates based on what you know you can afford right now. Additionally, some figures will be dependent on each other. For example, you could buy a used food truck fully outfitted with exactly what you need (or very close to it) for one price, or custom build a truck from the ground up for another price. I personally recommend comparing both options to see what will best fit your timeline, your budget, and your overall business plan.

If you are one of the many aspiring food truck entrepreneurs who is looking for financial backing, there are many options available to you.

The first option is financing through banks, credit unions, or other professional financial institutions. Depending on your personal financial situation and the interest of the bank, you will often be able to secure a loan with reasonable rates and terms. Often, you'll be able to find a loan at a reasonable rate and terms if you have worked with a particular institution in the past, or upon consolidation of several loans. If it's your first time having a "big" meeting with a bank, don't worry, it's not as intimidating as it might seem. Simply call up the bank and request a meeting to secure a small business loan, they'll take care of the rest. After the meeting, if it's clear that institutional financing isn't a possibility for you, it's time to consider the next option: private financing.

Private financing means raising capital from non-bank sources. This can be your friends, family, or anyone else you know who may be interested in investing with you. Each agreement and contract with one of these investors will be separate from others and you may need to find multiple private investors to reach your capital goal. Steer clear of handshake agreements. Put everything in writing, and it's preferable to have a lawyer review each one of your contracts. The advantage to private lending is that you can work out the terms of your agreement (the loan amount, interest rates, and repayment schedule) with an individual as opposed to a financial institution.

The third option to acquire the capital needed to start your business is crowdfunding. Crowdfunding is essentially asking strangers or your broader community to help you raise funding. There are multiple massive crowdfunding websites that exist for this very purpose. It can also be an excellent way to create buzz about your new business and spark some interest in your brand. Always investigate the specific terms of crowdfunding sources, some of them can be rather disappointing when you read the fine print.

There are also many resources available online, such as lending platforms, incubators, and Angel Networks. Lending platforms aim to help you secure a loan based on your business plan and budget. Incubators are good resources for connecting with other business innovators who can help you with more than financial support. They can also become mentors and help you learn more about your business along the way. Angel Networks are similar to incubators, with a focus on inspiration and support throughout the life of your business rather than strictly financial support.

The Legal Stuff

By "The Legal Stuff," I mean insurance, permits, accounting, and taxes. Due to the numerous variances in each state and even locations within a state, there's no easy way to condense this topic. But, they are each essential to running your business. You will find a bevy of links to help guide you through the particulars in the Resources section.

You will likely require commercial auto insurance on the physical structure of your vehicle, worker's compensation for your workers, as well as a business owner's policy, which provides liability coverage for your customers and coverage for your equipment. You can always contact your personal insurance agent for details as well. While they may not write commercial policies from their office, they should be happy to point you in the right direction. In almost every case, you will need a legally required amount of insurance for your business. If you have secured institutional or private loans, they often come with minimum insurance requirements as well.

Permits can vary as well, but you'll most likely need to have a permit from your local health department and a Fire Certificate from your local fire department in regards to that "hot, boiling grease" situation. You'll likely need a vendor or sellers permit from the state, a food handler permit issued in conjunction with completing a food safety and handling course, and both your business and your vehicle will likely need to be licensed with the state. Lastly, you'll need an employer identification number for the Internal Revenue Service (the IRS).

We've started the accounting process with the business plan and the chart shown earlier in this chapter, but this is really an ongoing process in which daily numbers become weekly numbers, monthly totals, and fiscal year finals. There are many software options available on the market today to help you with this process. Many digital Point of Sale (POS) programs have integrated accounting features so you can keep track of sales, profits, and expenses in real time.

Then there are taxes. If you are in any way unsure of what you're doing when it comes to filing taxes on your mobile food concession business, I strongly encourage you to contact a tax or accounting professional who has done this before. Given the threat of fines and imprisonment for falsifying, fudging, or even making accidental mistakes on taxes, I suggest everyone take this part seriously.

At this point, you can take a big, deep sigh of relief, knowing that you've made significant headway on the intricate, confusing world of paperwork and requirements surrounding your food truck business. You're not fully out of the woods yet, but you are in a very good position now. You know what you're cooking up. You have a good idea of your expenses, and you're on your way. Next, we're going to take some very big steps towards getting your business off the ground.

Chapter 2 Choosing Your Chariot

The moment is finally here! At long last, it is time to actually find your food truck.

You may have been scouring the sales pages online throughout this process. It's very easy to get swept away by some digital window-shopping. There are so many different options to look at. In fact, there might be too many.

So how do you narrow down the selection? How do you know whether a truck is right for you and your business? Do you choose a brand new truck that doesn't have anything installed yet? Or how about a slightly-used truck that needs a little love? Is there such a thing as the "perfect" fit when it comes to used food trucks?

Finding and Purchasing

The first thing you're probably wondering is "where do I even find food trucks for sale?" It used to be, generally, if you couldn't find one in the newspaper classifieds, you had to know someone who was retiring from the industry, someone who was upgrading or needed a different type of stand, or you bought a trailer shell and spent all of your time and money updating it from the axle up to perform its job adequately.

Today's food truck entrepreneur has two very exciting things working for them: the internet and the rise in popularity of the food truck.

In many ways, shopping for a food truck is like shopping for a car. There are many makes and models out there, and nearly all of them have some level of customization. Most of them are going to have the elements you need, but there are going to be some that fit your needs just a little better than others.

You are going to want things like a clean title, no significant accident history, acceptable fuel economy, and reasonable mileage on the odometer (if you're buying a full truck). Unfortunately, there's no Carfax-type program for food trucks, so you will have to ask questions like "has this truck caught fire before, and, if so, what was damaged?" or "have you had any major traffic incidents?" or "when is the last time you broke down, and what was done to fix it?"

You also need to consider everything inside the truck. Some friends of mine have compared running their food truck to being "equal parts auto mechanic, building contractor, and executive chef," and they're not wrong.

If you are not entirely comfortable evaluating the mechanical soundness of any of these elements, borrow some time from an expert, at least for the final purchase process. There can be a lot of hidden damages and problems that can quickly squelch your immediate plans for running a food truck empire. Having an expert who can identify them and recommend repairs can save you a lot of heartbreak.

Let's take a look at the different types of food service vehicles and some of the main points to inspect or consider when purchasing.

Pushcarts

If you're looking for a pushcart, your job is enviably more straightforward.

Your number one priority should be structural soundness. All of the wheels should turn without sticking or wobbling, and should move at the same rate. The axels should be supportive and rated to handle the weight of the cart itself. Any heating elements should heat, and any cooling features should stay cool. The drains and bins should open and not be rimmed with rust or have had rust obviously painted over.

You can make updates to cosmetic features with relatively little stress. The exterior paint can be changed to your brand colors. You'll likely want to post a menu as well. If the pushcart has an umbrella, sunscreen, or awning, they can generally be replaced if necessary.

Most pushcarts do not have a significant amount of wiring, piping, or power-operated features. If the cart you're looking at does have these features, be sure to inspect whether everything connects correctly and if there are any leaks.

Your bonus challenge is figuring out how to get it from place to place. Does it have a trailer hitch and significant weight so it can trail along behind a truck or SUV, or is it small enough that you'll need to load it into a heavy duty pickup bed or a trailer of its own? If it's attached to a bicycle, do you have the glute and hamstring power to bike it from where you will store it to every single event, or will you need some assistance to safely guide it up and down hills and along highways?

Trailers

Concession trailers can be tricky because many of them are retrofitted out of empty trailers, and as a buyer, you rarely have the ability to know who did the construction and whether they did it correctly. Hidden elements such as electrical wiring, gas fixtures, and floor reinforcement may require a thorough evaluation by a professional.

As a result, many food truck entrepreneurs are tempted to purchase their own brand-new trailer and customize it. There are many benefits to this plan, such as choosing exactly what you want in there and peace of mind that it's all correct. This plan is not without challenges, however. Generally speaking, this will be significantly more expensive, since you're buying brand-new fixtures, equipment, and perhaps paying for their installation. There are many skilled contractors and engineers who make their living building, remodeling, and updating food trucks and trailers. If you require professional help, make sure you have adequately budgeted to pay for these fees.

If you decide to do it yourself, you'll need a whole lot of tools, plenty of time, space, money, and a weather-proof place to store the trailer while under construction. If you have the skills and know-how to build your own trailer, it will be unforgettable and deeply rewarding. If you're not confident in your building skills, it's very possible that it will end up being even more expensive than if you had hired professionals.

If you're looking to buy a pre-owned trailer, here are a few things to check before you take the plunge:
- What is the trailer weight limit? What does it currently weigh, and will that change once you've added the generator/propane tanks/

- other equipment required for your specific business?
- How are you going to move it from location to location?
- Is it structurally sound? Walls, floors, ceiling, etc.
- How old are the appliances? Who installed them?
- Do the sinks, drains, ventilation hoods, lights, gas jets, etc. all operate correctly? If the current owner uses the phrase "there's a trick to this," your instincts to back away slowly are correct.
- Have there been any accidents inside the trailer or in traffic?
- Has the trailer recently passed a fire inspection?
- What size tires does it require, and how many? When were they last replaced?

There may be some less-than-perfect elements you're willing to accommodate or overlook, but that depends largely on your budget and your capabilities for making the necessary repairs or adjustments. If, for example, a trailer is perfect except you would rather have a prep fridge instead of an under-counter, this could potentially be a relatively easy swap. If you find a trailer that's in absolute pristine condition with everything you love, want, and need, but the entire electric system has been fried and needs to be completely rewired, that will be a much bigger project. Only you have the ability to decide if that's something you'd like to take on.

Trucks

Everything mentioned about trailers is relevant to trucks, with the exception of the towing bit. Since trucks have their own motor, you don't have to worry about how it's going to get from gig to gig...unless it's a real lemon. Therefore, I strongly recommend having some automobile expertise on hand when looking at truck options. When your car breaks down, it's incredibly inconvenient, potentially dangerous, and generally expensive. When your food truck breaks down on the way to a gig, you've got additional things to worry about, like lost wages, food waste, and a sullied reputation for flaking on a gig. Unless you, or someone in your inner circle, is a serious gear head, mechanical soundness is the top priority for your investment.

Hand-in-hand with mechanical soundness is structural soundness. Remember how the chuck wagons of yore were reinforced to handle the extra weight? That principle has not changed. You will be driving this vehicle on paved roads, grassy areas, gravel lots, and more. While it doesn't have to be off-road ready, it will need to be able to handle a few bumps, hills, and the mud.

Inside, you'll have the same checklist of considerations as the trailer and pushcart. Everything needs to function. Rust, corrosion, bugs, and rodents can be very difficult to overcome, but not impossible, if you're looking for a bit of a fixer-upper. Appliances can be customized and swapped out for something that fits your business better, but perhaps you can find a truck that doesn't need as much modification.

So where do you find these pushcarts, trailers, and trucks? I recommend scouring every online resource you can find. I've included a few in the Resources section to get you started, but there are many more options out there. I know a few individuals who have had great luck with online marketplaces such as Craigslist or eBay. You may have to travel to another state to evaluate your prospects in person, but if a road trip isn't your idea of a good time, you might want to reconsider the "mobile food vending" idea. Just like shopping for a personal vehicle, you'll want to look at a lot of options, compare features, weigh the benefits and challenges, and kick the tires a little bit before you pull the trigger on a specific vehicle.

General Maintenance

In the mobile food vending world, there are two significant emergencies that you want to avoid. The first is the truck breaking down on your way to a venue. The second is equipment failure in the middle of service.

As mentioned earlier, running a food truck combines a bit of auto mechanic skills, executive chef capabilities, and contracting work. You need to keep everything around, above, under, and in the pushcart, trailer, or truck functioning so that you are able to make it to every gig on time, serve your beautiful, delicious array of food to the expectant crowd, and return home safely.

There are so many things to remember that I've devised a series of checklists to get you on the right path. Perhaps not every item on the list pertains to you, and your county health and fire departments might have a few additional things to say, but this should get you started down a path towards a mindful relationship with regular maintenance for your mobile food serving business.

Truck Mechanics (for both food trucks and trucks pulling trailers):
- Are the tires inflated and ready to roll?
- Do you have sufficient fuel?
- Are you up to date on oil changes?
- How about fluids, including coolant, brake fluid, windshield wiper fluid, etc.?
- Any weird noises or smells?
- Do the brake lights and headlights work, the blinkers blink, and any hitches operate correctly?
- Do you have any chocks or braces for keeping the truck/trailer from rolling when parked?
- Do you have a spare tire? How about a roadside emergency kit?

For the cooking bay (or trailer):
- Are all cabinets closed and locked?
- Are all ingredients prepped and stashed in the correct spot?
- Have you brought along enough fuel for the generator and gas-powered appliances?
- Have the water tanks been sanitized and refilled?
- Do you have sufficient hand washing soap and paper towels?
- Are all the pilot lights in the correct position for travel?
- Are the windows, doors, and awnings closed and locked for transit?
- Have you accidentally left anything out and about that might rattle around during transit and damage things?
- Have you packed all of your signage and menus?
- Is your point of sale system on board?
- Do you have gloves, hair nets/hats, and aprons?

- When did you last check and replenish the serving gear and supplies?
- Did you clean every surface - floors to counters - before packing?

My MeeMaw would also ask, about ten to twelve times throughout the packing and hitching process, "what am I forgetting?" It might sound like a quaint saying, but I've found it really does stimulate the mind when preparing for a big event. It also forces you to repeat the checklist, and if you live with a heightened level of responsibility or paranoia, you may physically walk through the process again to make sure. This may seem like overkill, but knowing that an onsite health inspector can send you home over something as simple as not having your hair appropriately pulled back in a hat or hair net is usually enough motivation to inspire a heightened level of precaution.

In addition to regular maintenance and packing checklists, you will need to pay close attention to the overall cleanliness and structural integrity of your mobile food vending unit. One big risk that we've not yet addressed, and which you will hopefully never have to address, is infestations.
You do not have to be a dirty person or poor housekeeper to get roaches, mice, bees, or wasps (or whatever type of pests and critters are common in your part of the world). At some point, your trailer, truck, or pushcart will be stored somewhere, and pests will be more than happy to take up residence in a warm, dry environment. It is true, however, that they will be even more thrilled if you leave snacks for them, which is why I recommend cleaning your vehicle top to bottom before and after each event.

Some people store their serving gear and supplies in the truck or trailer when it's not in use. That's your decision, but remember, if you find signs of pests, *you have to throw it all away*. This serves as another argument for the plastic storage totes I mentioned earlier - the thicker, sturdier versions tend to be rodent-proof, which can prevent many unpleasant surprises.

Depending on where you live, you might have other uninvited guests, like bears, raccoons, opossum, lizards, snakes, and many more critters than I can possibly list here. While you may not prevent their curiosity, you can squelch their creativity by never leaving anything edible in your vehicle, and keeping doors and windows locked when your vehicle is in storage.

If you do find yourself with extra guests, the first thing you need to check is your local health ordinances for pest removal in food service. There may be specific regulations as to what measures you can take, such as types of traps, disposal of traps, and so on. Generally speaking, substances like rat poison are not encouraged in the food service industry, so always check before you take matters into your own hands.

Storing

One way to prevent infestations is by carefully considering what you will do with your food truck, trailer, or pushcart when it is not in operation. You'll need to plan for short-term storage, such as in between gigs, as well as off-season storage, in which you tuck your truck away for the cold or rainy season in your area.

For short-term storage, you really just need a safe place to park. This means security from pests, weather elements, and vandals. While a perfect location isn't always available, you want to do your best to prevent having to cancel a gig because your truck was broken into.

Depending on your community, you might be able to find space (or spaces, if you have a large vehicle) at a long-term lot, at your commissary, or in a storage facility with designated space for boats, RVs, and trailers. You may be required to drain/bleed any gas connections, clean and remove grease traps, and disconnect or fully remove fuel tanks and generators before storing your vehicle for liability and safety issues. Still, finding space for a 100-pound propane tank is much simpler than finding room for a 24 foot truck with 90-inch roof clearance.

Off-season storage is also something noted in the preliminary budget we compiled earlier. During the off-season, you'll have the bonus challenge of the truck not making any money, but still having its share of expenses.

Maintenance on your food truck is unavoidable. Just like anything else, you'll need to take good care of your pushcart, trailer, or truck in order to keep it working properly for a long time to come. Not only will this help you avoid an emergency in transit or at an event, but it will also help with the resale value of your business when you eventually decide to retire. Every aspect of planning a business is always about looking to the future.

Chapter 3 Cooking Up Connections

When it comes to taking care of, stocking, and operating your food truck, you can't do it all alone. Even if you're fully capable of biking around on your pushcart, you still need to buy food items and serveware so you can make sales. Therefore, you'll need to enlist the help of a few vendors and get some assistance. From food and supply vendors to staff and even commissaries, there are a few connections you'll need to keep your operation running smoothly every step of the way.

Suppliers

You will regularly need to purchase food, food service items, and cleaning supplies for your food truck. It is possible to source all of these items from the same location. You're likely familiar with purchasing dinner, paper napkins, and dish soap at the supermarket, so at the most basic level, you'll do the same thing for your food truck.

However, if you have simply decided that you'll run to the grocery store and just get "more" of everything that you usually purchase, you are definitely missing out on some potential savings.

Grocery stores and supermarkets are great. However, when it comes to providing high-quality ingredients consistently while providing significant savings, they are not the number one choice for those in the foodservice industry.

Most brick-and-mortar restaurant owners do not go to the grocery store every day. Instead, they have regular deliveries from food service providers. This allows them to ensure high quantity, high quality, and consistency across the board.

You are not a brick-and-mortar restaurant owner, and a giant delivery semi is not going to back up to your trailer and dump 25 pounds of tomatoes. Additionally, you may not have a place to store them. You also don't want to waste time and money driving around to find a store that has exactly what you want in stock.

You're going to want to investigate specific food service providers in your area. Some vendors have open warehouse type stores, where you'll be able to purchase bulk ingredients at restaurant prices without having to purchase a full walk-in cooler's worth of items. Some vendors will help you coordinate with a local restaurant as a drop point for your weekly delivery, which means you'll be able to place a regular order and then pick it up at a restaurant on a certain day. We have also explored the idea of entering into a relationship with a local vendor, which can help you bring that "farm-to-table" concept to life, while generating positive attention for both you and the farmer while keeping costs lower.

Since there are multiple options available, you'll need to do some research to determine the overall best fit for your food truck. There are two main factors you'll want to consider, which I hinted at earlier: quality and cost.

Quality is pretty easy to discern and can help drive not only what you choose to serve but what you charge. My favorite example to demonstrate this principle is the burger. A White Castle slider will set you back less than a dollar. While not the finest example of haute cuisine, it has a place in the world of edible items. The most expensive burger to date is a $5,000 wagyu beef, foie-gras-topped delicacy that is served with a rare bottle of wine. (I am referring to the Fleurburger 5000 of Fleur, a restaurant in Las Vegas. As of writing, it held the record for "Most Expensive Burger in the World.")

In each case, what you pay is directly proportional to the quality of ingredients involved. But at the same time, you have to look at the overall cost. The cost of a single food item is driven by how much the ingredients cost as a whole, and how much they cost per portion. This is why I asked you to write out portion sizes when we were creating prep cards in the earlier taco example. A White Castle slider is tiny and inexpensive, and basic ground beef is easy to source, which results in a budget-friendly product.

The general rule is your food cost should be around 30% of your revenue. To reach this figure, you will need to understand the math surrounding profit margins, and where to generate a return on investment. You also need to consider food waste. While it's not necessarily "waste" if you figure out how to use it in some manner before it goes bad, such as using those tomatoes from the taco truck to make chili at home, it's still cutting into your business budget, and is considered an overall loss. What you need to determine is how to buy the right amount at the right cost, and sell as close to that amount as possible for a price that provides you with, at the bare minimum, a return on investment.

My grandparents' popcorn is a great example of an amazing source of profit. As mentioned earlier, people pay far more for a large tub of popcorn than it actually costs. This is the methodology you need to apply when balancing your sourcing and your pricing. You can upcharge on reasonable items, especially in a "convenience" type setting. No one thinks they're getting fair food "at cost," but they're willing to pay $5 for an elephant ear because it's convenient, it's fast, it's delicious, and it's part of the experience.

When you're shopping for a food vendor, take all of these concepts into consideration. You might be able to sell a $5 hot dog out of a pushcart downtown after the clubs close, because there's nothing else around. If you attempt to sell that same hot dog at a fair where they're selling a $6 footlong corn dog two trailers down, you're going to have problems. But if that hot dog is suddenly made of free-range beef from Farmer Henry's place and topped with your specialty onion chutney, that $5 price tag suddenly makes sense again and, in fact, might even be a little low!

Food cost and price is variable, and it's often a concept that's hard to nail down into an exact science. I have friends with dozens of years in the food industry who still struggle with the fluctuations they experience. The most important thing to bear in mind when trying to shop for a food vendor that will help you adequately balance costs is that your portions, your quality, and your prices all have to appeal to the customer, or they simply won't buy. Shop around for the right food vendors to ensure you're getting the best price and quality.

The best bulk-food vendors are oftentimes the best service goods vendors as well. Fortunately, food industry suppliers know the game and are there to help you along the way. It's important to compare prices for napkins, cutlery, and serveware, but reliability is important too. Most food trucks will settle on one or two major vendors for the bulk of their supplies and food.

One wonderful added bonus for serving gear is that boxes of foil wrappers and unopened boxes of plastic forks don't have limited shelf lives, and will happily hang out in a varmint-proof storage option in your home, garage, or storage unit for just as long as you like. While ordering too much food results in food waste, these items can be tucked away and brought into service in your truck as necessary.

Staff

Staffing can be either the most difficult part of this experience or the easiest, depending on how willing your friends and family are to help you out. In my family, it was a foregone conclusion that each of us would spend the summers helping my grandparents with their concession trailers. Even as a very young child I would tag along, because my parents were often helping with the making and serving.

If you don't plan on making your food truck a family business, however, you will need to hire staff. Most food trucks operate with a staff of 1-4 people, depending on the size and complexity of the operation: each order needs to be taken, prepared, packaged, and served. Some food trucks hire a staff member strictly to work in the dish pit to continuously wash pots, pans, and equipment.

Hiring these individuals can be challenging. It's important for you, the employer, to have a semi-accurate idea of the number of days and hours you are asking your employees to work. If the service schedule is unpredictable, it's important to be upfront with your employees about this. Responsibility, flexibility, and adaptability are likely to be the qualities you're looking for in a candidate.

Another thing to bear in mind is that workers sometimes don't show up. Even the most conscientious, responsible worker will get a cold or have transportation issues. This may mean you have to fly solo during an intense gig, unless you have a few back-up folks you can call who are able to hustle to your location ASAP.

Hiring these individuals can be somewhat challenging, as you can imagine. You need someone who can work an unknown number of hours, an unknown number of days, in a location you may not determine until a few days before you head there. Not many people have that level of flexibility.

Instead, I recommend finding several individuals who can be on standby to work various shifts. If you have many people available at a variety of different times, you'll be able to schedule them appropriately ahead of time, so they're able to confirm availability or give you sufficient notice so you can make other plans.

The number of people you have in your employ can vary depending on how frequently you intend to operate your truck and your anticipated volume of sales per gig. Going to a brewery in the suburbs on an ordinary Wednesday night will be an entirely different scene than a weekend food truck festival in a large metropolitan area.

It will be helpful if these individuals are at least somewhat familiar with cooking, serving, and taking orders from customers, though these are certainly skills you can train. I encourage you to be fully transparent in your job listings as to the scope of duties they might encounter as well as the fact that this is a contract position, in which they are only paid when they work.

As for compensation, I'll keep this brief by saying you should always abide by your local, state, and federal tax and compensation laws.

In the meantime, you might put a few ads on local job boards or marketplaces. Remember that unless you plan on creating some seriously gourmet dishes, you're not hiring a Michelin Star chef. Instead, look for a responsible individual with good hygiene who can be pleasant to customers and take an order properly. Bonus points if they like the same driving music you do.

Commissaries

I've mentioned commissaries quite a few times, and unless you've had experience in the food industry before, you might be a bit curious as to what they are.

The term "commissary" refers to an off-site kitchen. Catering firms, food trucks, and even some restaurants have off-site kitchens where certain dishes or ingredients are prepared. You will need to pay for your space in this kitchen, which can either be a private kitchen or private kitchen hours, in which you have full run of the location, or a shared space, in which other vendors may also be in the kitchen at the same time, using the same appliances. There are designated commissaries, which you can picture as a large space full of different kitchen set ups, like a Home Ec. classroom, or a single, very large, very open kitchen. Sometimes, restaurants will have open hours in their kitchen space available to rent for a few hours for your prep, and some space for storage. Best of all, they are all up to code, fully equipped, and are health inspected regularly.

Why is this important? If you're running a hot dog pushcart, you'll likely not need a commissary. But if we head back to the taco truck example, there are many ways a commissary can benefit you. You'll have access to all of the space and equipment you need for prep and storage. Five heads of lettuce isn't a huge amount, but you'll have a tough time stuffing them in an under-counter refrigerator in your truck. Instead, you can keep them at the commissary, wash them thoroughly, drain them, and have a leisurely prep session, chopping a head at a time into designated containers that will fit in your under-counter refrigerator. You can season your ground meat early in the day and then return to portion it before taking the pre-portioned meat to your gig in the evening.

A commissary is where practicality and convenience meet for the food truck operator. You don't have to try to wash, strain, chop, prep, marinate, and so on in your truck if you have an off-site kitchen. You will have greater access to commercial kitchen appliances and supplies. This also opens up your truck's capabilities. Remember my friend Linda with the dosa truck? She and her mother-in-law meet at the commissary to prepare the batter, which can sit for up to 12 hours before being cooked. They pre-bake the pancake-like dosa at the commissary as well, because it can take up to 40 minutes for each one to cook. There is no way Linda would be able to bake each one to order with a timeline like that.

If you choose to explore this option, make sure you tour each commissary before you sign contracts. Get a feel for what you can and cannot do, how you'll be sharing the space, and who you'll be sharing with. You'll need to know the hours you can be there as well as whether you can actually pull your food truck up to load and unload there. It's a lot to think about, but it will save you so much trouble when it comes to preparing large quantities of ingredients on a tight timeline!

Chapter 4 Considering Your Operations Strategy

Now you've got your business plan. You're working on getting a truck that meets your needs. Your mind is racing as you choose vendors, set prices, and finalize all of the things that are needed to hand your food to a person in exchange for cash. The next important administrative duty is to put all of your processes and procedures together.

Processes

Remember those handy prep cards from earlier? They probably look a little worse for the wear at this point, with scratch marks, updated dollar signs, and names of suppliers jotted in the margins, but they're still incredibly important.

In order to make sure that everyone who sets food in your food truck or trailer is creating the same consistent product, I strongly encourage you to write out and prominently post instructions for everything that happens inside the truck. That includes preparation, cooking, taking orders, serving, cleaning, and even using the point of sale system.

The notes that were on the prep cards for the tacos make the perfect basis for these notes. You should only make these instructions as complicated as they need to be to get things done. For example:

COOKING MEAT FOR TACOS
1. Remove one portion of meat per taco from the refrigerator.
2. Place portion on a clean, heated grill surface.
3. Allow meat to cook for 2 minutes on one side, then flip. Allow two minutes on the second side.
4. Ensure meat has reached a temperature of 165 degrees Fahrenheit. Use a meat thermometer.
5. Serve immediately.
6. Wipe down and scrape grill top immediately before preparing the next order.

This is just a hypothetical example, of course, but it's the type of procedure that everyone can easily follow. This ensures all of the items you sell turn out as close to identical as possible. Use this type of instruction to create easy-to-follow recipes, explain which foods go in which wrappers or containers, and even the order in which the person at the window takes an order, calls an order, and rings it up in your system. If everyone is doing everything the same way each time, you'll have fewer errors, a faster service time, and everyone will be happier- you, your staff, and your customers.

Of course, we are all human, and we make errors. One of the top causes of errors is allowing substitutions and alterations to orders. Have you ever ordered a sandwich with no dressing but ended up getting a sandwich with dressing anway? In the fast-paced and cutthroat world of food service, an incorrect order can be a tragedy. Even if the customer is happy to wait for you to fix the mistake, re-making an order in the middle of a rush can be catastrophic for the other customers' wait times. Some food trucks, and even restaurants, have strict "no substitutions" policies to circumvent the problem all together. In fact, of the 14 food service experts interviewed for this book, all of them begged me to recommend "no substitutions, EVER!" You can create a work-around for substitutions if you have a written ticket system or plan to print receipts. Start by either taking the customer's name or giving them an order number. The ticket shows the customer's entire food order with any substitutions or special requests. This ticket is then placed in a docket holder in view of the chef while he prepares the order. When the order is cooked, the chef places the food and the ticket to the packaging station. While packing, it's a good idea to label the bags, containers, or trays if possible to stay organized. When handing the order to the customer, it's not a bad idea to reiterate the order, as well, if possible.

No matter how you do it, having a well-defined process for organizing orders and getting them to the correct customer is essential. Every person in the food truck should know this process by heart.

Set Up, Serve, And Strike

You'll also need a series of processes and procedures for set up and strike (tearing down and packing up) as well as keeping things running in between.

In some cases, one individual (usually the owner) is in charge of specific tasks, like set up. That includes parking the vehicle, stabilizing it, opening the service window, unrolling awnings, hoisting the overhead flags, setting up any condiment or serving tables, and so on. You'll also need an indoor prep person to get everything staged appropriately, turn on the grill, stove, fryer, and any other equipment that needs time to warm up before use. Depending on how long your gig is, you may need to change out fuel tanks, feed the generator, wash dishes, etc. If the weather changes, you may need to make adjustments to your awning and lights. You'll want a point person available to speak with the health inspector (again, usually the owner).

Afterwards, you'll need to strike everything. That means turning off the gas and generator, wiping everything down, cleaning and putting all of the dishes back into storage, draining the grease, securing all equipment, collecting trash that has blown around the truck, and more. You'll also want to take end-of-night inventory, though you may wish to do that when you drop off the remaining food items at the commissary.

Having a detailed checklist of all of these procedures will help keep things moving smoothly throughout the duration of your gig. It will also help you meet the expectations of the health inspector and ensure that nothing is ignored.

Safety

There are a few special safety considerations that must be kept in mind when operating a food truck. Between the generator, appliances, fuel sources, and other hazards, there are some elements of a food truck or trailer that can become extraordinarily dangerous under the right circumstances. Food trucks do occasionally blow up, and grease fires are unfortunately pretty common.

As you prepare to take your food truck on the road, you must be prepared for all of the various emergencies that can occur in one. This is not to say you need an advanced degree in medicine. Instead, make sure you have a comprehensive first aid kit on board as well as a fire extinguisher sized appropriately for your appliances. Check out the National Fire Prevention Association guidelines and recommendations for food trucks, and post reminders for your staff where they can all see it.

While prevention is key, and your maintenance of the truck will help prevent a lot of issues, you must be prepared for the following calamities:

- Grease fires
- Engine fires
- Generator failure or fire
- Propane tank failure or combustion
- Heat exhaustion
- Human injury, such as burns and cuts

Whether your state or county health department requires it or not, both you and your staff need to be familiar with safe food-handling practices. There are several online courses that can be taken and posters with safety guidelines that can be discreetly posted where your staff can be regularly reminded. Working in a food truck can be very fast-paced, and things can just happen without anyone being to blame or at fault. Being prepared to deal with each of these issues as they arise will make the experience so much better for everyone involved.

The administrative side of your food truck business may be less "fun" than the food-service side. Just keep in mind that it's the administrative side that allows the food-service side to thrive. If you don't pay your vendors on time, screw up the payroll, aren't prepared for safety issues, or get shut down due to improper permitting or health standards - you won't ever be able to get to the "fun" stuff at all.

Throughout this section, hopefully you have revisited your notes, including your prep cards and budget table, and modified them along the way. You may have created what you thought was a final business plan, only to find a better option. You may have several different versions for several potential situations, such as various food vendors or multiple truck options. I encourage you to continue to work with all of these details over time in order to keep a conscious eye on growth and performance. While profit margins are often slim in the first year, your business will only continue to grow through vigilant attention to your costs versus profits. While you can read about these details here to prepare, there's really nothing like plenty of real-life experience.

Section 4 Turning a Business into a Brand : Establishing Yourself and Making Profit

If you consider the process of building your food truck empire as a checklist, you are now very close to the end. But this doesn't mean you're "done" or that you can rest on your laurels, knowing you've done everything you could. The process continues and, in fact, I'd even say the process never ends. Let's take a moment to look at how far you've come so far:

- You've learned about the history of food trucks, and different types of opportunities you can pursue.
- Then you started planning your business by deciding on what you'll make in your food truck.
- Next, you considered what type of equipment you'll need to make and serve that particular food.
- We looked at how food trucks are equipped with water, gas, and electric.
- Then, we hunkered down and put everything we'd learned into practice by creating a business plan.
- Your plan led to the hunt for the perfect food truck, storage space, and commissary.
- You worked on creating all of the processes and procedures needed to safely operate the truck.

The last step is the continuous work of building your brand and getting people to come to your food truck. In this section, we'll take a look at marketing, branding, and other things you can do to ensure your business gets all the customers you deserve.

Chapter 1 Building Your Brand

When you apply for your permits and Employer Identification Number, you've got to include your business name for tax purposes. Granted, the name on the side of the truck doesn't have to match the name of your business, but chances are good that you started brainstorming this way back when you decided the type of food you'll serve. Coming up with a name is very personal, but the best options make sense to your customers, are easy to remember, and align with the experience you want your customers to have. Linda, for example, named her dosa truck after her mother-in-law, Aakshi. "Aakshi" is a traditional South Indian name that pays tribute to her partner in the kitchen.

However, building a brand is so much more than coming up with a name and the colors you'd like to paint your truck. Your brand should convey:

1. The type of food you serve
2. The experience you want your customers to have
3. Your brand values

You might be thinking "The experience? What does that mean? I want them to buy tacos and walk away!" True, but there's a little more to it than that.

There's a reason why brick-and-mortar restaurants spend thousands of dollars on decorating, carefully select the music, and hire friendly waitstaff. They're creating an atmosphere or "experience." Food trucks are different. They are inherently *part of* an existing atmosphere: a music festival, a state fair, a wedding reception, or even just a pushcart on a boardwalk at the beach. The hard work of creating an atmosphere has already been done for you. It's your job to take advantage of it.

All the atmosphere in the world, however, cannot overcome a poor food experience. Just because a customer's favorite band is playing at the main stage of a music festival, they will still notice if you serve them bad food. The foundation of all customer experience is the product itself.

Building your brand can happen through the little things, like a friendly yet professional staff and serving food quickly. You don't have to have the biggest flags, the loudest music, or the flashiest menu. You just have to make people happy.

The best way to make people happy is by giving them exactly what they want. In order to do that, you need to know your audience. This might change gig by gig, but it's important to know who is coming to your truck and what they're likely to buy.

- **Demographics** is knowing who your customers are. That includes age group, location, and what they like. Knowing that you're pulling up to a very formal business where everyone will be wearing suits may limit your ability to sell sloppy joes, for example.
- **Geographics** is knowing where your customers are. Understand your location with practical details that might influence buyers. It's unlikely you will be successful selling ice cream to children at a construction site.
- **Psychographics** is knowing what your customers want. It involves tapping into the subconscious of your customers to understand why they buy what they do. Folks working at a construction site might be less interested in having an international culinary experience, and more focused on having a hearty meal that will give them the energy they need to wrap up their project.

As you consider what the people want, always remember what *you* want.. Do you want to try to take the truck out as much as possible, or do you want this to be a fun weekend side hustle? Are you planning to make this your vocation for the rest of your life, or are you building up your empire until it makes sense to sell it? Are you really interested in traveling as far and wide as you can, or do you want to be a fixture in your community?

Your answer to all of these questions will determine how you market your brand. "We go anywhere!" will appeal to a far different audience than "Your hometown taco truck!"

The expectations you set for your truck will determine how you market and sell your brand. The good news is that you can technically change and adapt during the lifetime of your truck. Businesses are constantly re-branding and altering their plans - you'll just need to make sure the effort you're willing to put in is equal to your end goal.

Chapter 2 Designing Your Marketing Plan

Your marketing plan only needs to be as robust as you want it to be, and that you feel you can consistently maintain.

When someone hears that a food truck will be coming to their area, they immediately do an online search to learn more about the truck and the menu. You may choose to have this information posted online via a website or via social media. There are benefits and challenges to each, naturally.

With a website, you can really "set it and forget it," as the saying goes. You can have a very simple website that displays a few pictures of your truck, lists the menu, and maybe spouts off a quick mission statement and/or history of the truck. Most importantly, you need to have a number or email address where people can contact you to book your truck.

Aside from making sure the information on that site is true, such as when the menu or prices change, you don't really need to do anything about it. People won't love it, but they'll have the information they want. You might get several business cards from web developers who buy your wares, happy to help you build something more robust, but that decision is yours. Your website can be an interactive wonderland with all sorts of features, games, videos, and more, but it's not required for the purpose of providing information.

With social media, you have the same opportunity to upload pictures of your truck, add your menu, and some basic information, but you also have a duty to participate in the interactive nature of it. Many food truck owners use this to their advantage, updating to share their location for the day, any specials on the menu, and so forth. They use the process of frequent updates to keep a buzz of excitement going about their business. As mentioned earlier, one of the specific challenges to having a food truck was the difficulty in finding repeat customers, as folks will have to find you. If your social media account says "come see us at Place 1 on Monday, Location 2 on Tuesday, and This Other Event on Friday," you have just opened the door to people lining up on all three days, if they so choose. And they might just so choose!

Anything you do on social media can be done on a website, of course, but if you choose to make social media your primary online presence, you really must update it every week at minimum. There are many reasons for this. Primarily, you want to stay in people's feeds. Facebook, Instagram, and other social media platforms have an algorithm that chooses what people get to see when they log in to their own profiles. If you don't update regularly, your page will just... disappear from their feeds. Additionally, some social media outlets will shut down an account or become suspicious of a user who doesn't update very often. With so much fraudulent activity, it's easy to understand why they do this. But as a business owner, it's a huge pain to re-establish everything once it's been removed.

My personal recommendation is to create a website and a social media presence, but only if you have time -- or a trusted assistant -- to keep social media updated. You do want people to find you, and you want gigs to book you. Honestly, in the digital age, having a way to contact you and see what you offer is very necessary.

You can also choose to be included on a variety of different apps. Most cities have a site that rounds up all active food truck permits. Some of these sites also allow you to link to your website or social media page, and update with future appearances, too. Some apps even track locations on a daily basis, and if your truck is operating that day, will provide users with a map to your service window.

Technology can be very helpful for getting the word out about your food truck, but it does often come at a cost. Before you say "yes" to every app that comes calling, double check the listing fees, and make careful note of what you can get out of the experience. If you're going to be doing private gigs, for example, you won't be able to invite the public, so that would be a moot point. On the other hand, if you're going to hit new locations around town every day, you might be exactly the right candidate for listing on a "find my truck" app.

Advertising might be in your wheelhouse if you are actively looking for gigs and bookings, or if you plan to be in a single location for several days or weeks. As a marketing professional myself, I could wax on for an entire series about advertising a food truck business, but for the sake of brevity and staying on focus for this book, I'll keep it simple. And honestly, that's the best advice I can give you, as well. Facebook ads are relatively inexpensive and low-risk, and are a great way to temporarily generate buzz when you have a big event coming up, or when you're looking for bookings for the next season. Placing your digital business card on local news sites, community message boards and marketplaces, and advertising your presence at certain locations or events throughout the year is also a great idea. But you don't need to go full Google Ads Campaign for a taco truck that operates once a week. That was part of the reason you chose this business model, after all!

Also, I can't stress enough how much plain ol' low-tech word of mouth can do for your business. This is why you want to have a memorable brand, because people will tell each other about your food, your truck, and your business. "We had the most delicious tacos at work the other day. The truck was called (insert name here), and they had beef from Henry's farm! I even picked up a coupon to order beef from Henry directly!"

Even the most basic hot dog pushcart can take advantage of word of mouth marketing. "I was walking down High Street after paying my bills at lunch, and I couldn't figure out what I wanted to eat. There was this hot dog cart at the park there at the intersection. $5 got me a dog, can of soda and a bag of chips. It was perfect. Here, I got the guy's card with his website."

As these examples demonstrate, people will remember excellent experiences. They will tell other people. They will retain this information, and any marketing you do beyond that, such as websites, social media, apps, and more, will simply keep that memory alive.

Chapter 3 Selecting Your Venues

How do you choose where you'll appear? How do you know where hungry people will be? As you're now aware, getting the truck out and prepping food for the masses is a lot of work, so you don't want to put in all that effort to sell one measly taco.

Evaluating venues can be tricky, because there will always be a first time and there will always be exceptions to every rule. There will be times when you have to close early due to running out of everything, and there will be times when you can't even give away food. There may not be any specific rhyme or reason to this.

Here's an example of how inconsistent the experience can be: I recall one rummage sale my grandparents dragged us to in the spring. It was cold and murky, but in the spirit of rummage sales, the place was packed. My grandparents' trucks were the only options for onsite food all day, from 8am to 8pm. At the end of the day, we'd sold lots of coffee and plenty of cold drinks, but very little hot food. Even with the sweet smell of cinnamon wafting through the grounds of the sale, we sold less than a dozen elephant ears in as many hours. That memory sticks with me as the perfect example how crowds can be very unpredictable.

You have a choice as to what venues you'd like to book. Would you like to show up to feed drunken party-goers after concerts or when the clubs close? Do you want to book exclusive gigs, like being the only food truck at a brewery or event? Do you want to do the fair circuit? Perhaps you find appearing at corporate locations and businesses during lunch break most appealing. You can do any or all of these, but remember, each one has a particular audience. Always refer back to the demographics, geographics, and psychographics of your potential customers before reaching out to venues and potential gigs.

If you live in a highly-populated area, it may seem that food trucks are everywhere these days. We've come a long way since the days of the chuck wagons and roach coaches following cowboys and blue collar workers from place to place. You can find food trucks at parks, gas stations, rest stops, and anywhere tired drivers might stop to grab a snack. Food trucks appear at sporting events, car sales, and even at private events like weddings for family gatherings.

Only you can decide which options will work for you and your food truck. You'll need to provide the food and the staff. You'll need to appear at the designated time frame. It's up to you to evaluate the effort and cost versus the payout.

There isn't one set business model to describe the relationship between food trucks and venues. When appearing at private events, you may charge a flat rate to rent your business for the day. Some events or locations may offer a symbiotic relationship, such as parking at a brewery or business. They don't pay you, you don't pay them, and everyone keeps what they make on sales. Alternately, you may have to pay a flat fee or a percentage of sales to appear at certain events, such as fairs or food truck festivals. In these instances, you're paying for exposure and essentially buying potential customers.

No food truck is guaranteed a great big profit-making day. As you work more and more gigs, you'll start to see what works and what doesn't work. You're going to find yourself experimenting a lot. Things will change as you try to find your stride. You will spend money doing things that will never earn you money but, unfortunately, you won't know until you try.

The first year or season may be difficult as you attempt to find your niche. You might make some decisions that you'll look back on with regret, but always consider these learning experiences.

Conclusion

In the introduction, I mentioned that there are many decisions that need to be made, and that every decision will lead to more decisions, which may cause you to re-evaluate your entire plan. At the time, that might have sounded like an exaggeration, but at this point in the journey, as you look over your corrected and edited notes, you might just agree with my initial assessment.

When you started this book, you might have had a very clear vision of what you wanted to do. But as you worked more and more towards the reality of your own truck, things like budget, equipment needs and costs, or the difficulty in securing local permits might have caused you to rearrange your plans, edit your decisions, and put a sad end to some dreams.

I would ask you to not give up on those dreams. Just because you don't have the funds right now, or because a particular business model doesn't make sense right here, doesn't mean you have to give up on it forever. New opportunities arise all the time. Keep those notes. Keep those dreams. And look for just the right moment to jump, armed with all of the knowledge you have gained by reading this book and trying things out for yourself.

The future of the food truck industry is what you and your generation make it. In the COVID-19 era in which this book has been written and published, more and more food trucks are finding a place to park on a permanent basis and offering delivery, either through a website or through apps like GrubHub and UberEats. Some are making regular appearances in neighborhoods, since there are restrictions on crowds and restaurants. The most frustrating part about business is that no two days are the same, but that challenge is also the greatest benefit for innovation.

Your food truck empire may not grow exactly as it did in your dreams, but your intelligent planning, your insight into your market, and your ability to provide the customers with exactly what they want will ensure it becomes exactly what it ought to be.

May your wheels stay on the road, your cooktops stay warm, and your customers love every bite!

Resources

As mentioned throughout the text, there are a lot of things that you'll need to research on your own, whether related to your specific location or your truck's individual needs. To help you get started on this path, I've rounded up a few online resources. I'm not affiliated with any of these sources in any way, and I'm not specifically endorsing anything, either. These links are provided because the information contained in them may be helpful to those getting started in the mobile food vending business.

Food Truck Facts

As a "business geek," I like to look at facts and figures surrounding an industry before I dive in. I like to get a feel for what the market is like, so I can plan accordingly. These pages provide insights into common food truck statistics from around the United States.

"25 Powerful Food Truck Industry Statistics in 2020"
https://2ndkitchen.com/restaurants/food-truck-statistics/

"U.S. Chamber of Commerce Foundation Food Truck Index"
https://www.foodtrucknation.us/wp-content/themes/food-truck-nation/Food-Truck-Nation-Full-Report.pdf

"12 Impressive Facts on the Food Truck Industry"
https://www.food.ee/blog/12-impressive-facts-on-the-food-truck-industry/

Vehicle and Fire Safety

Your food truck will need to pass a fire inspection, so you'll want to be aware of requirements. It's also incredibly important to know about the risks of fire or explosion for your own truck or vehicle.

"List of National Fire Prevention Association Codes & Standards"
https://www.nfpa.org/codes-and-standards/all-codes-and-standards/list-of-codes-and-standards?mode=code&code=96&tab=editions

"Food Truck – Propane and Fire Safety"
http://foodtrucktrainingcertification.com/articles/food-safety-news/food-truck-fire-safety/#:~:text=Propane%20tanks%20are%20convenient%20and,like%20any%20type%20of%20fuel.
https://www.nfpa.org/codes-and-standards/all-codes-and-standards/list-of-codes-and-standards?mode=code&code=58&tab=editions

Food Safety

Food safety and proper handling is a requirement for every food truck owner or staff member who handles food regularly. Certifications may be required as well, depending on your city or state. Here are some resources to get you started with learning more about food safety training and proper food storage and handling.

United States Department of Agriculture "Danger Zone" (40 °F - 140 °F)
https://www.fsis.usda.gov/wps/portal/fsis/topics/food-safety-education/get-answers/food-safety-fact-sheets/safe-food-handling/danger-zone-40-f-140-f/ct_index#:~:text=%22Danger%20Zone%22%20(40%20%C2%B0F%20%2D%20140%20%C2%B0F)&text=This%20range%20of%20temperatures%20is%20often%20called%20the%20%22Danger%20Zone.%22&text=Never%20leave%20food%20out%20of,or%20above%20140%20%C2%B0F

The ServSafe Food Handler Program
https://www.servsafe.com/ServSafe-Food-Handler

StateFoodSafety's Food Handlers Card Training
https://www.statefoodsafety.com/food-handler

Financial Guidance

If you are interested in pursuing a business loan or financial assistance for your food truck business, here are a few leads you might wish to pursue. Again, this is not an endorsement or indication of affiliation, but a few common resources for small business owners and start-ups.

Small Business Association
https://www.sba.gov/

Connections to investors and lenders for your area, your business, and your ideas
www.prosper.com
https://www.facebook.com/trustleaf/
www.ondeck.com
www.lendingclub.com
https://www.loanbuilder.com/lb/dm

National Business Incubation Association: A global network of resources and mentors for new business owners
https://inbia.org/

Angel Networks
https://www.angelcapitalassociation.org/
https://www.angelinvestmentnetwork.us/

Crowdfunding
www.kickstarter.com
www.ourcrowd.com
www.indiegogo.com

Insurance
Food trucks have their own unique insurance requirements, since they are both a business and a vehicle. These resources can help you find a quote or learn more about your insurance options and needs.

https://www.fliprogram.com/food-truck-insurance
https://www.insuremyfoodtruck.com/
https://www.thezebra.com/insurance-news/5173/food-truck-insurance-101-coverage-need/

Employer ID Number

Food trucks in the United States will need to contact the Internal Revenue Service for their official identification number. Get started here:

https://www.irs.gov/businesses/small-businesses-self-employed/apply-for-an-employer-identification-number-ein-online

Taxes

Tax regulations and requirements differ wildly, so be sure to check your location's tax filing instructions specifically. To get you started, however, here are two articles that I found helpful.

"Food Truck Tax Basics"
https://mobile-cuisine.com/taxes/food-truck-tax-basics/

"Tax Tips & Deductions for Food Trucks"
https://smallbizclub.com/finance/tax-and-accounting/tax-tips-deductions-food-truck-owners/

Accounting Software/ POS Software

In order to keep track of funds, inventory, taxes, and staffing, you'll need a great accounting system and an easy-to-use, accurate point of sale system. These links provide reviews of various software options that are ideal for food truck and mobile food businesses.

Accounting
https://www.softwareadvice.com/resources/opening-food-trucks/
https://mobile-cuisine.com/accounting/finding-the-best-food-truck-accounting-software/
https://quickbooks.intuit.com/industry/restaurants/

Point of Sale
https://www.softwareadvice.com/retail/food-truck-pos-comparison/
https://fitsmallbusiness.com/best-food-truck-pos-systems/
https://toppossystem.com/food-truck-pos/

Health Codes

Health inspections are common when you run a food truck business. Be prepared by learning the requirements you must meet before you hit the road.

United States Food & Drug Administration "State Retail and Food Service Codes and Regulations by State"
https://www.fda.gov/food/fda-food-code/state-retail-and-food-service-codes-and-regulations-state

US Small Business Administration "Apply for licenses and permits"
https://www.sba.gov/business-guide/launch-your-business/apply-licenses-permits

Vehicle

Buying the actual food truck can be incredibly nerve wracking. Here are a few sites that offer information and advertisements for trucks currently for sale. You can use this information to get ideas, shop for your truck or trailer, and get an idea of current prices in your area.

https://roaminghunger.com/start-a-food-truck/
https://www.usedfoodtrucks.com/
https://foodtruckempire.com/buy/
https://concessionnation.com/shop/food-trucks/
https://www.webstaurantstore.com/article/487/food-truck-design-and-layout.html
https://www.trailerfactory.com/custom-food-trucks/

Commissaries

The following sites can help you locate a commissary or available kitchen shares in your area.

https://www.thekitchendoor.com/
https://foodtrucksuppliers.mobile-cuisine.com/supplier/real-estate/commissaries/

Reviews

Reviews and feedback help improve this book and the author. If you enjoy this book, we would greatly appreciate it if you could take a few moments to share your opinion and post a review on Amazon.

www.ingramcontent.com/pod-product-compliance
Lightning Source LLC
Chambersburg PA
CBHW071420070526
44578CB00003B/633